MANY
MANY
BEGINNINGS

By
Cem TANRIÖVER

"This is an innocent fairy tale…

send it to everyone you LOVE!"

-CEM TANRIOVER

DEDICATION

It is with my deepest gratitude and warmest affection that I dedicate this book to all mothers and fathers around us who are or have been a constant source of wisdom and inspiration for all of us. The following pages below provide a way to honor anyone who does not want to forget but remember that peace and respect are possible for all of us. We are created for fellowship, to form the human family, existing together because we were made for one another, including those living with Alzheimer's or Dementia.

TABLE OF CONTENTS

ACKNOWLEDGMENTS

This book is based on research conducted on colorful murders. I am grateful for many great spirits, friends, and colleagues in encouraging me to start the series – Not So Innocent Fairy Tales, preserve with it and finally, publish it. With gratitude to Mothers, Fathers, Artists, Writers and Poets, Teachers, Scientists, Psychologists, Sociologists, Architects, Protectors of Justice, Green Economists, Protectors of Humor, Critics, Thinkers. Special thanks to:

Adam Smith, Albert Einstein, Ali Alper, Ali Sevil, Alkım Gülcan, Antoine de Saint-Exupery, Aristotales, Aristide Maillol, Arthur Miller, Auguste Rodin, Aysel Gürel, Barış Eliş, Barnett Newman, Bernard Lacroix, Bernard Maris, Bernard Verlhac, Bernd Raffelhüschen, Brian Greene, Can Bayhan, Tom Moore, Carl Gustav Jung, Charles Aznavour, Charly Wittock, Chico Mendes, Christian Hans Andersen, Clarissa Pinkola Estes, Constantin Brancusi, Constantine P. Cavafy, Çetin Aktaş, Damla Sevil, David Carus, Desmond Tutu, Edward Said, Emile Zola, Engin Önbayraktar, Ernest Hemingway, Erwin Schrödinger, Fahrettin Tanrıöver, Fahrettin Demirkaya, Fatma Tanrıöver, Feriştah Sevil, François Marie Arouet (Voltaire), Frank Lloyd Wright, Franz Kafka, Gabriel Bjerke, Garri Bardin, George Floyd, George Ivanovich Gurdjieff, Georges Wolinski, Gerhold Blümle, Gerry Pack, Gustav Vigeland, Gülçin Aktaş, Gülenbaht Şentürk, Günter Knieps, Halil Güner, Helen Keller, Heinz Mack, Henri Poincare, Hermann Hesse, Isaac Asimov, Isaac Newton, Jack Zipes, Jean Arp, Jean Cabut, Jean Jacques Rousseau, Jean Moulin, Jean-Marc Cosyns, Jean-Paul Sartre, Jerry Pinkney, Joanna Brady, John Baldessari, Kader Sevinç, Klaus Ludeloff, Knut Hamsun, Léon Foucault, Malcolm X, Marcel Proust, Maria Filomena Fernandes-Teixeira, Marie and Pierre Curie, Martin Heidegger, Max Frisch, May Sarton, Maya Lin, Melinda Berlant, Monad Balkan, Muazzez İlmiye Çığ, Mustafa Kemal Atatürk, Narriman Narrisol, Noam Chomsky, Oliver Landmann, Onur Sarısaban, Oktay Sinanoğlu, Oswald Spengler, Otto Piene, Otto Rank, Paula-Irene Villa, Pablo Picasso, Petter Andre Rommen, Philippe de Coune, Philippe Honore, Plato, Richard Feynman, Robert & Ruben Oppenheimer, Sabine Hark, Salim Aktaş, Sarah Elkington-Auberge, Sema Dayı, Semiha Berksoy, Sezen Aksu, Sigmund Freud, Sokrates, Soner Canözer, Stefan Zweig, Stéphane Charbonnier, Tankut Öktem, Thomas Mann, Thomas Paine, Turhan Selçuk, Van Bryan, Verena Seißinger, Victor Hugo, Werner Heisenberg, Yedi Bilgeler, Yoyo Maeght, Zeynep Aktaş, Zuhal Önbayraktar. And to Old Friends.

When

OUR INNER CITIES

were created with a separation of opposites and the sun became
distinct from the moon, then came the high tide on human spirit which
was there left alone, alone to search for
unity.

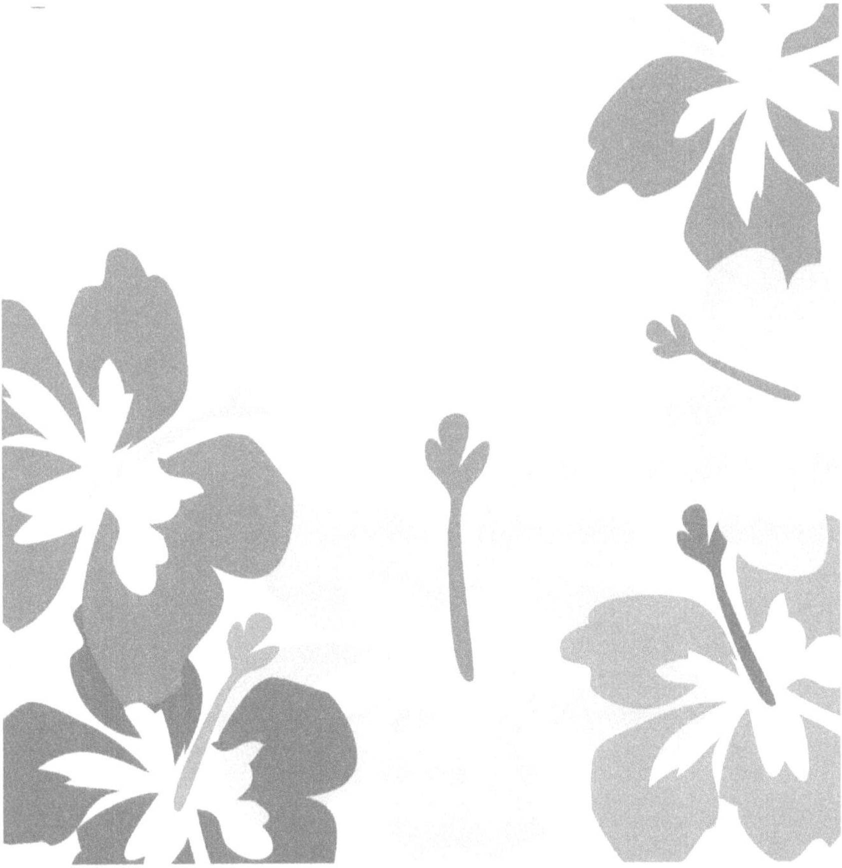

JUST FOR YOU!

This
blank page is
meant just for you.
It is intentionally left blank
as an open invitation to come back to it
once you have read the book until the end
so that you can make a symbolic drawing
that will always remind you of
A GENEROUS LIFE

1

THE CHILDHOOD

WHEN A BULLET starts its short journey, it always obeys its pre-determined trajectory. And one out of a million times, the final destination of its trajectory is your head. When such a bullet is headed towards your head there is not much time left for you to think about things. Your wife, kids, your parents, or how you wanted to change the world can suddenly become obsolete.

Even if you are cool enough to remain calm by just the look of someone firing the gun, you would consider yourself lucky, if you can get to see the face of the shooter not because the bullet flies quicker than the speed of the motor-like sensory mechanism of your cognitive capability but because those

shooters mostly never intend that you uncover their identity and are disguised and probably have worked long-hours if not trained a lifetime to catch you off-guard.

In such unpreparedness -a juicy target for every killer- there is not much left which prevents you from looking like a fool. They win and you lose. But this is not the saddest thing of it all. Rather it is the choice of a tabloid editor preparing the headlines for its reader, who is expecting it and is ready for it! Only if you are lucky enough your bloody picture with a hole in your head is the headline that makes the headlines.

At least then your wife, children and parents have a kind of consolation. But what about me, the guy who does not belong to this close family circle, and is not interested in mafia stories or never had heard about this man with the bloody picture? A conceptual murder, so what, why shall I care at all?

***

P aris, 20h33,

31 December 2018,

Lying next to each other on the couch, they watched the movie. In the film, the Native people who fought for 200 years for land, life, family and the right to be free, said:

"Put down your gun, let's sit together. If you lower it, friend, we talk about peace, we will deal with you. When they lowered their weapons, we murdered them. We lied to them. We tricked them to break their land. We sentenced them to hunger, so that they forcibly sign those papers that we were never loyal to and called treaties. We turned them to beggars on this continent, which had only lived long enough for life to remember. And no matter how you interpret the history, distort it no matter how much you distort it: we did not act correctly. We were neither fair nor honest. We did not have to return their rights to them, nor to stick to our treaties. Because the supremacy of our power gave us the right to attack the rights of others, to usurp their property, and to just take away their lives while trying to defend their lives and freedoms. While their virtues turned into crime, our immorality became virtue. "

Forty-five years had already passed. At Le Taillevent, an elegant restaurant close to where they live, they chose their most stylish outfits for a candlelit Christmas dinner. The choice of the restaurant was in line with the spirit of celebration, as Le Taillevent offered modern elegance, assertive cuisine and a remarkable wine list.

All night long, they talked about the good things that the new year will bring, as if they were trying to suppress the echoes that echo in the ears of the movie they just watched on the couch.

"But there is something this heresy cannot reach, and that is the great judgment of history. Be sure that history will judge us. But do we care? What kind of moral schizophrenia is this, we cry out that we have fulfilled our commitments until our lungs exploded with the voice at the top of our nation for the whole world to hear, and all those hungry, thirsty days and nights that the American Indians have spent over the past 100 years say the opposite of what this voice says."

Right in the middle of the night, to the crowd to watch the New Year's show at the Arc de Triomphe, in the middle of Charles de Gaulle Square, promised to be the most unforgettable of all time, with an excited wait like not only Paris but all of France and even Europe. they confused.

Then they drank drinks at Le Duplex, one of the famous nightclubs on the famous Champs Elysées street, very close to Arc de Triomphe. When they finished the second goblet, everything was like a clock that worked perfectly for the hottest lovemaking of their lives - except for something they didn't know.

At 5:30 it was nearly impossible to take the call and answer the insisting telephone, due to heavy alcohol and all the partying of the long night.

It was his mother on the line.

"Jimmy, you need to take the first flight back home. Yesterday afternoon, your father had a heart attack, and we spent the whole night at the hospital. He is in a coma," she continued without being able to hold her voice the way as he always remembered her in his ear.

"You must come as quickly as possible because…"

***

ONCE UPON A TIME, there was an orphan boy without shoes. But he collected all the pieces of fabric he found and after a while, he sewed a pair of blue shoes. Their appearance was coarse, but he loved them. Even though the days passed by gathering food in thorny woods until the weather got dark, the shoes made him feel rich.

He loved walking with these blue shoes all day long. He walked day and night and loved to sing a particular song, called THE PUZZLE. His legs were as strong as a tree trunk. Like when sometimes children pose basic questions, he often was murmuring its lyrics and lulling everyone else around – who would be embarrassed to ask such questions - to dream:

Every time defaults anew

My memory

To earths coming

The earths leaving

Who am I really?

He was a vibrant boy, filled with seemingly unlimited sources of energy. He would spend most of his time alone. His friends in the village called him 'Jonas, The Old-Fashioned Boy'. There was something inherently subversive and utopian in him that kept his friends returning to him throughout their childhood lives, hoping that he might open the portal to another world.

It was right there, the old village where they all got to know each other.

Every time when playing together in the lush gardens of their primitive village, they recreated the world anew. Taking what was and combining it with what was possible, they were happy. The Old-Fashioned Boy was radiating to his proximity a sense that he may bring something new and special into the world, a magical sense of hope that everyone nourished inside to make the world a better place. As such, he embodied the principle of innovation and transformation that underlies every single creative act that has occurred in the course of civilization. In those days, his village hung lilacs right up to the windows, even to his humbly furnished room. Back then, they were living in the age of exploration. They ate only once every two days.

One day he found a small pouch with various herbs and a note that was left for him at the door of his cousin's house. It wrote: Drink this, have your will. 'The Old Fashioned Boy', who did not mind trying, prepared a tea from these herbs. Then he drank it with pleasure. While enjoying this herbal tea made from marjoram he believed that he will also enjoy good fortune soon.

Meanwhile, the discovery and conquest of new lands, overseas expansion, and new trade routes kept constantly changing their lives. Every time 'The Old-Fashioned Boy' was about to miss his real family, he would go on for a tour and walk. Upon his return, he sometimes would visit the grandparents of his cousin Jack. They always loved to talk about how to prepare for one's own future, especially about how to lead a proper life, telling short stories about the good and the evil.

One evening he involuntarily heard them talking about him, proudly mentioning how they had managed to provide good schooling for 'The Old-Fashioned Boy', even though he was an orphan:

"This boy will be well educated and he is really smart. He is a good boy. Soon he will be a very important businessman and marry the most beautiful girl in our village." they were whispering.

When suddenly a tremendous wave of writing and circulating fairy tales for children emerged, no child in their village was spared. He enjoyed his long walks, which ended sometimes passing by his cousin's house. There Jack's grandparents would provide him warm healthy food and read to him those fairy tales. This became almost a routine. Yet, every time he listened to those fairy tales, he found something odd in them: They were mostly told in such a way as if to assure he would be properly groomed for the best place in their community.

Left without a choice, he started to pay more attention to the stories which cultivated in a moral envelope. The more fairy tales arrived at the village, the less he wanted to go to his cousin's house to listen to them because after each session of reading, he gradually realized that somehow his soul was turning into a wilderness - with all the complexity about upper and lower classes, the mixture of good and evil, and the conflicting motives found in these stories.

Meanwhile, other children, who did not question those fairy tales, have acquired a wide range of technical skills that enabled them to come up with marvelous strategies and inventive solutions for dealing with the increasing pressures their village placed on them to cope with everyday responsibilities.

All days seemed the same as they grew together.

THE COMPETITION

Meanwhile fierce competition for trade and empire among many villages led to the widespread adoption of selfish policies. In the coffeehouses there were some who waited for glory. Although with empty stomachs, they never ceased believing.

Everyone sought to increase their wealth and power by obtaining large amounts of gold and silver and by selling more goods to their neighbors than they were buying. The increased richness in gold and silver flowing into their village led to a price revolution, which encouraged trade and businesses of all types. But these developments never cast a shadow on 'The Old-fashioned Boy's reputation for his avant-garde playfulness.

"To live here without belonging to anything, but still involved with everything takes a lot," he thought. His social and artistic conventions were only occasionally matched by his friends. He still preferred to gather with Jack and his parents around the stove to recite verses in exchange for a warm meal.

Nevertheless, as prices of goods went up, his friends were willing to take risks to invest money in the hope of making more money. This new attitude spurred the growth of his village, where the elderly enjoyed a high degree of power, for it was they who possessed the traditional wisdom of the community, the kinship lines that prescribed marital ties in obedience to extensive incest taboos, and techniques for survival that had to be acquired by both the young and the mature members of the group.

Yet, he decided not to place himself at the mercy of this technical storm but tame his inner world as a cultural being. Thus, he kept walking and singing in his blue shoes, nevertheless being wary of the attempts to thwart his need to play and dance through the formal high-pressures of his village.

SOMETHING HAPPENS

With the rise of other villages, a shift from blind custom to a commanding morality, and finally, to rational ethics occurred. After beginning to read about ancient times 'The Old-fashioned Boy' found a new source of inspiration. He learned that if one way does not lead to the desired direction, to take another. He read about how the ancients thought about things which at first looked dark.

Meanwhile he was growing fast, too. His biological event of puberty unleashed a powerful set of changes in his adolescent body that reflected themselves in his sexual, emotional, cultural, and spiritual passion. Suddenly he found himself looking out to reconnect with his deepest inner zeal for life.

He dreamed about marrying the girl of his life, imagining their friendship basking aglow in the spangled light of the sun.

One day Jack's grandparents told him:

"You see, we don't have mushrooms and embers. We can't go to the forest because we are old. Jack cannot go because he is afraid. You are the only one, who can go to the forest and find mushrooms and get ember to fire our fire again."

"All right, okay, I'll go, "

he answered to Jack's grandparents.

The forest was far from his village and the road was narrow. and its road was narrow. As soon as he started walking, he got into the darkness and slowly disappeared. The branches, which were broken under his feet while walking, suddenly frightened him. So he sat for a while and stretched out his hand to touch his blue shoes and thought:

"Just touching these blue shoes makes me feel better."

THE NEW NORMAL

Each time the road within the forest bifurcated, he would consult his shoes.

"All right, should I go now left, or right? "

Blue shoes guided him,

"Yes," or "No," or

"In this way," or

"In this way."

When he finally collected the mushrooms and the ember, he had already moved very far deep in the forest.

Where exactly was he now?

He realized that he had come very close to a point that not many dared to go. His throat tightened. The path was dense, packed with too many obstacles to count. He was almost to their neighbor village. Suddenly he saw someone moving!

It was a girl. Yes, it was a girl in white, who passed on a horse galloping in front of him. Horses of this breed were often bred for use in races; it was rare to find one in the forest.

The air enlightened. He instinctively followed her, walked, and walked quicker, and finally when he approached her, the sun began to shine. It was the first time that he forgot about his blue shoes and his village, for a while.

Jacqueline was pretty, gentle, and charming – just like in those stories Jack's grandparents had been reading to him. She was dressed very well. But would she like him?

She like everybody else of his friends was immediately inspired by his magical appearance, yet she knew how to control herself at all times.

'John, The Old-Fashioned Boy' was attracted to her, but there was a small problem. She was not from his village. So, he promised her to come back and marry her, once he would settle things back in the village.

THE POINT OF NO RETURN

Rushing to return to his old address as quickly as possible, he delivered what Jack's grandparents had asked him to do. Yet his timing was not good. He arrived much earlier than expected.

At the time being, the members of his village were far away from gradually disengaging themselves from the biological facts of blood ties, to admit 'Jeremy, The Old-fashioned Boy' as a stranger, to increasingly recognize him as a shared community of human beings than of kinsmen. They became even furious when he told them about the patient and beautiful Jacqueline – the girl from the other village. Not approvingly, they asked 'James, The-Old Fashioned' boy for obedience – without any room for discussion.

Not impressed by this intolerance 'The Old-Fashioned Boy' had to choose how to respond and make up his mind. Did he want to keep his ability alive to respond to whatever situation he might face in the future or did he want to surrender to the comforts of the village? It seemed to him that this was something everybody in the village should make up their minds on.

"They do not understand me! I should think for myself and never do something just because others are doing it. Most of my friends belong here but they are not involved. For them belonging is just their insurance policy."

He looked at the lilacs hanging out the window. Having to choose between the girl he wants to marry and his traditional roots, he felt pain. But his pain oddly made him also self-aware. There was something else why others regarded him as a stranger.

Since he was born others were calling him with different names. His name kept changing every time as his behavior was changing and his consciousness was reaching new heights. It looked, as if he was blessed with the right balance of both a mystical and supernatural reinforcement that was always accepted by the other members of the community.

Now, thinking about these things calmly, he watered his lilacs in the window for the last time, being assured that he had nothing to fear about. He should go on to marry the girl of his dream, assuming that, also there, in the new village, he would be welcomed.

THE RIOT

Determined to take a hold of his life, he prepared a tiny luggage. One night, he silently left his native village with a light heart. After crossing through the forest, he was thrilled to see Jacqueline again, who was indeed waiting for him right there where he had left her. Happily, 'The Old-Fashioned-Boy' married his love and started a new life in his father village.

For many reasons time seemed to pass quicker there. The discovery of new machinery and advancements in farming introduced far-reaching effects. The use of new crops and techniques, and the introduction of better methods of soil rotation enabled to grow more food. This helped to raise the standard of living in 'The Old-Fashioned-Boy's father village. This revolution provided the food for the expanding populations in all villages and directly led to a population explosion in the whole community.

Soon he realized that on the contrary to his native village, his new village appraised thrift, saving, and even parsimony as virtues, for only by these means could capital be created. They provided a favorable climate for the early development of a new age, with its promises of profit. 'The Old-Fashioned Boy' was not prepared for it.

"Everywhere I see winners and losers. I observe landless laborers, white servants and Negro slaves, employed by prosperous farmers and merchants and artisans. This belongs to this class. This belongs to that class. No one lets himself be helped!"

Reminding himself that being alive requires an effort far greater than the simple fact of breathing, he felt as if his fellows in this new village were dying, in small doses within themselves, as the sun sets each evening.

One evening he argued with his wife Jacqueline. He was a very difficult man for a woman to live with. By quieting the wheels of her mind, Jacqueline tried to relax her body and said:

"I cannot imagine who could be a good wife to you." fighting back tears and often repeating herself, she found these words:

"Please, we can get along here! Once you fall in love, you can't escape if you run away. The more pleasant it is to love, the harder the separation. We all can get along here. I mean, we're all stuck here for a while. Let's try to work it out."

'The Old-Fashioned Boy' eyes moisten, yet he was not impressed. In the evening sitting together at the stove, they barely speak a word to one another. With his eyes looking outside through the window, he thought:

"She does not understand me! No partner in a love relationship... should feel that one has to give up an essential part of oneself to make it viable. Once the words are out of the mouth, it is difficult to make up."

He started to imitate the trees.

Soon, they broke up and that is how he learned to lose in order to recover, and remember nothing stays the same for long, not even pain.

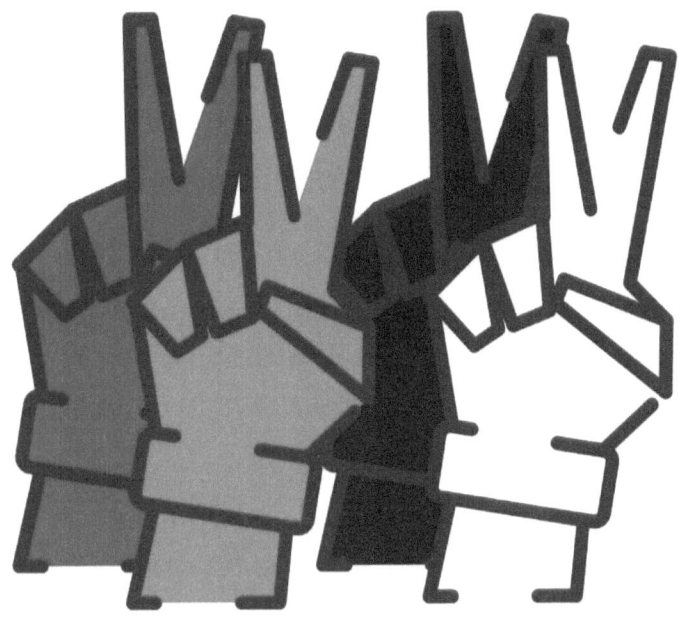

P aris, France 20h33,

06 January 2015,

Strong beliefs in white self-determination and empowerment can be dangerous.

On January 7 the office was the target of a terrorist attack. At 11:30 AM two brothers, armed with assault rifles, entered unnoticedly the door of the office and first killed caretaker Mr. Boisseau. They then obliged Coco to enter the secret code that granted access to the upper floors, where an important meeting was being held. The attackers rushed into the meeting room, and a police officer, who had been assigned to protect the office, was shot before he had the chance to draw his weapon. The two brothers then asked for Charb and four other fellows —Cabu, Wolin, Tignous, and Honoré —by name before firing fatal bullets towards them as well. Their other victims were economist Mr. Maris and psychoanalyst Mrs. Cayat, and journalist Mr. Renaud, a guest at the meeting. "We won. We killed them. They lost!", they shouted triumphantly as they ran through the streets, escaping in the darkness.

A race started to find out who the responsible was. A race that looked nothing like those before.

Yet, the attack on the office and the massacre of twelve was the first in a series of assaults that was going to claim more than two hundred other lives since January 7.

It sent shockwaves through the globe, exposing divisions in the multicultural modern republics around the world and initiating a fierce debate about intentions and true intentions. About facts and fabricated facts. About cultivating and manufacturing consent. At the heart of these discussions were the role of consciousness: united consciousness through art, literature, and even press freedom, against an invisible enemy, dividing consciousness.

In France and other countries around the world, some were talking about social, ethnic, economic, and geographical 'apartheid' and grim inequalities as the root of the problem.

"We must ensure that solidarity, which was expressed at the time of the funerals of those 12 lives, attended by more than 1.000 mourners, remains as strong as ever,"

everybody shouted in the northern town of Bernay.

From then on, nothing would ever be as before!

But after a while, human beings started to forget day by day. They went – back to business - as usual as they restarted to sing:

"Mamma Mia, here I go again!"

22

2

THE APPRENTICE

A BULLET flying towards the head of the victim does not necessarily cause immediate death, though it very often does.

It depends on the gun used, the ammunition it was shooting, and exactly where the bullet hit and where it traveled after hitting. The speed of the bullet will be around three hundred meters per second. It will take about one out of two thousand of a second for the bullet to traverse the brain.

During that short amount of time, experts assume that pain signals will transmit at the normal speed of nerve impulses, about a bit more than half a meter per second. As brain matter has no nerves, the signals of pain will come from the area where the bullet enters and exits. Consequently, it will not have time to reach the pain receptors on the brain before death or before consciousness ceases.

So, no!

You won't experience any pain.

* * *

NOW, once again he was alone. First, he started to walk, reflecting on his blue shoes that had guided him to come to this village. Time was calling him now to move away.

But to where exactly?

Instinctively he decided to return to his old village before dawn to see if everyone was safe. It had been a while that he did not visit his friends. By the time he arrived, he was surprised to see how time had changed everything, even the architecture of his native village. He could not find where Jack's grandmother's house was located. Trying to bring back the memories of his lilacs was to him as if coming at sea with a dense fog.

His mother village around him buzzed with energy. On every corner, there was a rush. He had always enjoyed his walks through the commons, where he would occasionally meet his lively and joyful friends who now seemed to feel very different.

The village was just plagued by hierarchies and class structures which tended to acquire a momentum of their own and permeate much of everyone living in it. So too the market began to acquire a life of its own and extended its reach beyond limited regions into the depths of vast once unknown continents.

Indeed, the notion of progress, once identified by the ancestors of 'The Old-Fashioned Boy's grandparents as faith in the evolution of greater human cooperation and care, was now identified with economic growth.

As the evening arrived, he anxiously was looking for a shelter as he heard a familiar voice shouting at him!

"'Jason, The Old-Fashioned Boy'! Is that you?"

"Yeah, it's me, old is gold right?"

he answered his cousin Jack, who was now married to Jacqueline and responsible for hacking the forest between his mother and father villages into fuel for iron forges.

He felt all alone like a branch of a dry tree. A by that time unfamiliar, strange mix of feelings, relief, happiness, and sadness flashed him at the same time.

His fondness chased rather by the question: Yet, who have they become and to whom was I evolving... was this question supposed to provide relief? ...initiated so many pictures of himself which have just flown in front of his eyes trying to catch moments.

"What happened to our village?" he asked him dazzled.

"I can't believe it has been so long!" Jack answered.

They sat down for a moment. On the one hand, they boiled a plant called marjoram from the herbs that they had previously gathered, which is good for the soul, as well as the stomach as they were sipping it in a wood fire, and remembering those joyful days with their old friends.

"Things changed from the time you left 'Joseph, The Old-Fashioned Boy'," Jack continued:

"Important as greed or the power conferred by wealth, maybe, sheer survival requires now that an entrepreneur must expand his or her productive apparatus to remain ahead of other entrepreneurs and try to devour them. The key to this new law of life -to survival- is expansion, and greater profit, to be invested in still further expansion. What one says achieving is, my friend, a high art you will understand."

"I see,"

he replied, even though he felt that he and Jack no longer possessed a unified consciousness.

"Jack does not understand me!" he thought.

For him Jack was living like in a state of hypnotic 'walking sleep' in front of machines that would take down more trees. He instinctively saddened. Somehow the bond between the two best friends seemed to be broken and from now on they had to live apart. For this, he better had to make a good plan, as, in this age of industrialization, he never knew how to handle with greed or selfish power.

SUBPLOT

Jack sensed that 'Jamal, the Old-Fashioned Boy' was somewhat resentful of his status. But what could he have done alone?

What would he have changed?

The transformation from an agricultural to an industrial society had long influenced political, economic, and social structure.

The landed aristocracy, which had begun to lose influence because of the rise of the middle class, would be completely overshadowed by the birth of the new capitalist class of businessmen.

The seismic shift from a rural society to an urban society, self-made wealth replaced the inherited power but created enough new problems, such as how to deal with the conditions created by the factory system.

ALL IS DIFFERENT NOW

It seemed that all human relations have shifted.

After many years in young adulthood of following the scripts of his mother and father villages for creating a life, he was a kind of lost in midlife.

Alone, without his wife or a family nor his old friends who got ahead with life and had, unlike him, now lifelong responsibilities.

What was 'The Old-Fashioned Boy' supposed to do?

He was almost sure that Jack and his grandparents would call this a crisis, conjuring images of how 'The Old-Fashioned Boy' was engaged into outrageous and impractical things, leaving first his native village, then the second one and finally his beautiful wife, etc.

As bad as those images were sounding, he knew deeply that all was ok, he just was undergoing a midlife transition and it's not all bad.

He felt he needed time.

To avoid being depressed, he looked at his blue shoes and decided to walk again. By walking he could cure himself and take a break from worldly responsibilities to reflect upon the deeper meaning of his existence.

A NEW UNDERSTANDING

"How could all his fellows stay where they are, since the only real nature of human beings is that they never stay at one place for too long?"

he asked himself.

After a while, 'The Old-Fashioned Boy' could better forge ahead with new understanding. By that time many of everyone's certainties were undermined: mercantilist trade reduced to one-way street; human individuality reduced to an instinctive sex drive; fossil evidence showed that the Earth was much older than the estimate based on scripture; and that even the most deeply held ethical principles were simply constructions. They were something that was not inherently natural, but created by society. For the elderly they were an extremely important concept in the social life because without them, their neighbours would not be the same. The constructs very much shaped lives. But now more and more started also to shape them.

He realized that villages, communes, identities and culture were very important issues but mostly, their division and control was arbitrary, unless they had a connection with being a human. He thought:

"If the existing society changed, new constructs would develop and old ones may weaken."

This element of contemplation represented now an important resource that he could draw upon to deepen and enrich his being.

Gradually, everyone, he met started to call him 'Jonny, The Apprentice.'

THE PLAN

The more he gazed at what remained from the forest, the clearer the pollution became to him. His fellows were causing tremendous stress on themselves as well as on the ecological system. To his surprise, most of the people with whom he has talked about these issues in the village have told him that they did not think that this was a good thing either. Some even confessed that their lives were not meaningful enough. It was difficult to find answers. Fellows seemed not to know themselves. What they were sure of was their names given by their parents. Yet, no one including 'The Old-Fashioned Boy' could know what a good life is until being disposed to pursue it.

"Nothing can be good unless it is pleasant on balance,"

he reflected.

For a good life, should he then engage in following a philosophy of the aesthetic, the life and art in harmony with nature?

This would mean that the proponents of growth and development would battle with him on how to find the middle ground and lessen the impact of industrialization on the environment. But the debate and fight would probably never end, because for him, there would be no middle ground.

The environment had to be protected!

He took a deep breath:

"My community should not consider it an honor of how much spontaneous vegetation it destroys; it should rather be a point of honor for every community to protect as much of its natural landscape as possible."

Yet, to engage in ecologically sound practices those times placed a morally concerned entrepreneur at a striking, and indeed, a fatal disadvantage in a competitive relationship with his old fellows. Notably with those, who lacked any ecological concerns serving to a naked idea: To produce at lower costs to reap higher profits for further capital expansion, totally ignoring dead birds, farm animals, and fishes.

Yes, smelling, dead fishes, which had become a common occurrence around.

THE NEW HABIT

As he continued walking longer, he developed a habit of playing with salient ideas. Now on the vertical axis of life, a striking thought compelled those forces that once had bowed down to wake up again.

He self-confessed about children:

"Since children are family members who are the first to be taken as examples in the development age, the attitudes and attitudes of the parents to their children are internalized by their children and they show similar behavior when they grow up."

Was the child-parent relationship clear in Jack's family?

The attitudes and harsh behaviors that will be taken against the child negatively affected the psychological development of the child and cause them to experience lack of self-confidence. If children were not raised in a consistent and understanding manner, they would not have benefited them at first, and would not have had much benefit in the family and society.

"How many parents were there to encourage their children not to be identified with their parents?"

"Plato,"

he remembered. If he was next to him, he felt that he would support him:

"A democratic environment should be created within the family and a family order should be established by setting certain rules. It means that the pursuit of happiness is natural and innocent and that morality which tried to impose upon all of us a way of life, by which in general the man, who follows it, has to sacrifice his well-being must be wrong."

He took another deep breath:

"We need to cultivate the human being. Every human being is capable for a unique possibility. A child should not be a legacy."

Of course, mother and father were to love their children unconditionally and make them feel it. Who was his own family?

For the first time, since 'Johnny, The Apprentice' had resumed his life as a single, he started to feel good again. Solitude had provided an important aspect for his creative thought and answering questions one by one seemed to relieve him:

"We need to cultivate the human being. We need to cultivate the human being in such a way so that the intrinsic intelligence and being 'human' is more important than being influenced by this or that."

He wanted to be more precise about -this or that – but suddenly it started to rain:

"MODERNISM, WITH ITS FRAGMENTED VISIONS OF THE WORLD AND ITS INSISTENCE THAT THERE IS NO SUCH THING AS AN OBJECTIVE PERSPECTIVE, WAS A BLOW AGAINST THE SMUG CAPITALIST STRUCTURE OF ADVERTISING AND CONSUMPTION."

"Some say that creativity offers purpose, while others believe that virtue, or moral life, confers meaning. But every time I take a walk, I feel fulfilled as if rearing children with love or making an intelligent discovery. I think values are made just by us in our minds and subject to change over time. The one who persists is a person of purpose,"

he repeated.

Yet he had to mature before such a blow could be managed and would free others from the illusions about the essential.

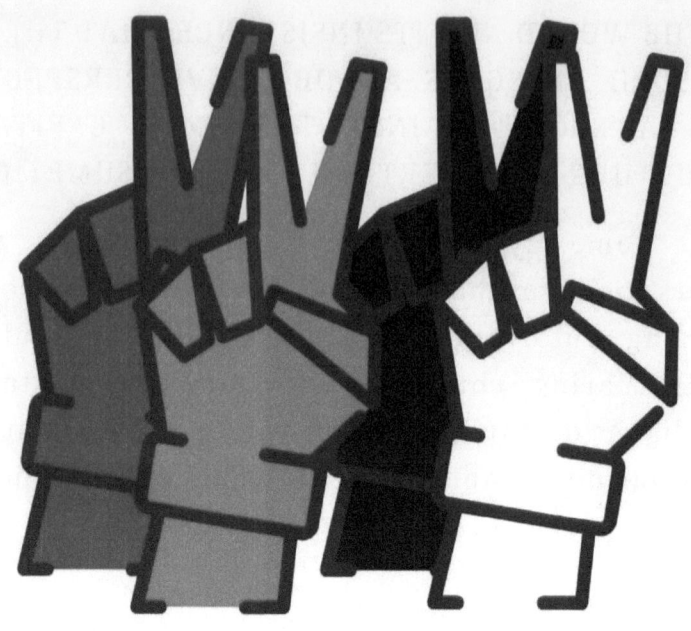

New York City, U.S.A. 20h33,
20 February 1965,

Strong beliefs in black self-determination and empowerment can be dangerous. Two days before his speech to be held in the Audubon Ballroom, he told interviewer Mr. Parks that a group was actively trying to kill him, as if to reassure that the more articulate a person is, the more dangerous words become. February 21, he was preparing to address his audience in the ballroom when someone in the 400-person audience shouted,

"NIGGERRR!

Get your hand outta my pocket!!! "

As he tried to calm the disturbance, suddenly a man rushed forward and shot him once in the chest with a sawed-off shotgun and at the time the first bullet was sent onto his trajectory two other men charged the stage firing semi-automatic handguns.

He was pronounced dead at 3:30 pm, shortly after arriving at the hospital. The autopsy identified 21 gunshot wounds to the chest, left shoulder, arms, and legs, including ten buckshot wounds from the initial shotgun blast. One gunman, was beaten by the crowd before police arrived. Witnesses identified the other gunmen. All three were convicted of murder and sentenced to life in prison.

The attack in the ballroom was the first in a series of assaults that was going to claim more black lives since February 21.

"The first time I saw those bullet wounds,"

Mr. Parks thought,

"Why doesn't someone want to get to the bottom of this?"

Everyone started asking questions. What was the real story?

In the USA and other countries some were talking about social, ethnic, economic, and geographical 'apartheid' as well as grim inequalities as the root of the problem.

"We must ensure that solidarity, which was expressed at the time of the funeral, attended by some fourteen thousand to thirty thousand mourners, remains as strong as ever." everybody shouted. For the funeral, loudspeakers were set up for the overflow crowd outside Harlem's thousand-seat Faith Temple of the Church of God in Christ, and a local television station carried the service live. From then on, nothing would ever be as before!

But after a while, human beings started to forget day by day. They went – back to business - as usual as they restarted to sing

"Mamma Mia, here I go again!"

3

THE MATURE BOY

WHEN GUNMEN shot someone in the head, the victim has a better survival chance than someone who is targeted at the heart. Ensuring enough oxygen and blood supply to the brain is decisive to survival.

Firstly, survival from a hole in the brain depends on the location of the brain in which the bullet strikes. If you are lucky, you can have a situation, where the brain's ventricle is not so badly struck, so that the cavity may be avoided from filling with so much blood to cause the brain to swell dangerously.

Secondly, a victim has a better chance of survival if the round misses the major blood vessels, avoiding the situation, where a lack of enough oxygen to the brain can be fatal. Therefore, the velocity and caliber of the bullet as it travels through the brain make a huge difference.

If the victim continues to breathe and their blood pressure remains stable, then the victim has a good chance of survival.

Nevertheless, if a bullet passes through both the right and left hemispheres of the brain, instead of either the right or left hemisphere, then the damage will be harder to repair. This is because the brain can - to a certain degree- recover the loss of either hemisphere. One of the hemispheres can compensate for the damage of the other, but when both hemispheres are damaged, compensation is nearly impossible.

So, what makes a person die on the spot when shot in the head?

A large caliber round at close range which strikes the ventricles of the brain. Add to that, the police taking forever to reach the scene of the assassination. It is the ideal combination that will surely cause any victim to die.

***

"**WHAT** makes a human life have meaning or significance is not the mere living of a life, but reflecting on the living of a life,"

he reckoned;

"Unlike a bullet, which never betrays its pre-determined trajectory, we can change our point of view on any given situation. When we choose to do so, the facts remain the same, but a deliberate shift is made in how we see them."

As the evening arrived, he heard an affable voice shouting at him!

"'Jamie, The Mature Boy', is that you?"

He looked back and saw Jack and Jacqueline together, hand-in-hand.

"Yeah, it's me, old is gold right?"

he answered his cousin Jack, holding the hand of Jacqueline, who was now in charge of philanthropy. Following their passion, it seemed that, Jack and Jacqueline were not alone.

"Just a little greeting, what is this longing for? Come on, let's make peace."

Ever since they last met, Jack and Jacqueline had gone after their passion. He learned that likewise a few of his old friends had already started to go under a deep transformation as well. Especially those in mature adulthood, who have raised their large families, well-established themselves in their work-life, and became contributors to the betterment of everyone; through volunteerism, mentorship, and all other forms of altruism.

"I would've never thought we'd meet again. I thought everything dies along with the time that passes," he inhaled.

A familiar, great mix of feelings, joy, happiness, and excitement flushed 'Jamie, The Mature Boy' at the same time.

COMING TOGETHER

They sat down for a moment. On the one hand, they boiled a plant called marjoram from the herbs that they had previously gathered, which is good for the soul, as well as the stomach as they were sipping it in a wood fire, and remembering those joyful days with their old friends. Their past was coming back from the bottom of its defeat:

"I can't believe it has been so long!"

Jack and Jacqueline explained briefly everything that had happened:

"Joy, happiness ... we do not question. They are beyond question, maybe. A matter of being. But pain forces us to think, and to make connections ... to discover what has been happening to cause it. And, curiously enough, pain draws us to other human beings in a significant way, whereas joy or happiness to some extent, isolates."

Suddenly the night fell and the air got cold. However, they quickly overcame it alongside some other problems, such as the concentration of power perceived as autocratic and dangerous for individual freedom and democracy. Reassuringly, after overcoming those problems, such as the concentration of power, understood as autocratic and dangerous to individual liberty and democracy, they, as soon as the sun rose again, had started to live together for a sustained period of time with great benefits; broadening education, transportation, and human rights with reduced hunger and malnutrition and the advance of science.

Slowly yet, miraculously welfare states emerged with institutions for healthcare and education along with direct advantages given to individual fellows through pension systems and social insurance.

Everyone benefited now from their benevolence and solidarity, including those outer-directed fellows who loved conformity.

'Jamie, The Mature Boy' was impressed by Jack's friend's change, especially by their decency, commitment to honesty, and intellectual curiosity. For him, now, Jack was awakened from the state of hypnotic 'walking sleep'.

He smiled, murmuring to himself:

"Now I understand them!"

Now he was happy to have a good example in the vicinity of his life that some in the commune were trying to uplift others. The influence, generated by what benevolence said and did, had as much an effect—if not more—over his development as his fellows.

"It is a pity that I did not have someone close to me before as a good example uplifting others. Much of what's good in me will one day come from this, and I count myself lucky to have the beneficial effects of this influence over me."

He next found himself wondering about the power of influence in general.

"What could I do myself, so that others could learn from my example one day to be able to give more of themselves to others, too?"

'Jamie, The Mature Boy' asked Jack.

"You can help others to elevate energy-stealing thoughts into more responsible ones, such as: 'I think there must be a key, something important for me to learn here. We become what we think about," replied Jack.

Thinking about it together, they began to realize that it was they who had to learn so much more in the first place.

They began to listen to the conference of the birds, among the forest. Yet they had to hurry up. They had to be quick because each single day the forest was diminishing and resources were getting scarce. The resources were getting scarce at an unprecedented pace.

Despite growth, not every fellow was lucky. On the contrary, rampant commercialization and globalization had left many behind, while the malign era of 'Transaction Man' had already extracted fellows' wealth and became ruthless in his view of social obligations. Finally, the ecological damage was now forcing the descent of man.

THE SACRIFICE

As time became important, they first discussed the issue with time:

"If we don't make better use of our time and meet our small goals, layer by layer, then we'll never achieve the bigger ones that are most important to us," they concluded.

Then they had a conversation about what it takes, sacrificing stability and leaving oneself with unpredictability, to follow one's dreams.

"How can a person, starting from nothing, who has no particular advantage in the world, reach the goals that he feels are important to him, and by so doing, make a major contribution to others? "

he asked loudly.

"Each one of us has their responsibilities and sometimes we simply have to compromise with others. If we don't learn to say 'no' or give up what is not essential, we are the ones who suffer at the end."

By the time they raised the next question,

"What do we have to give up today for a better future?"

inter-generational arrangements had already changed the world once again into a totally different one; this time led by giant technology firms that were seeking to overthrow the old order with platforms that have millions of connected people. Though these were only digital connections. Their spiritual bonds as counterparts based on consent and mutuality, was largely missing. Consent was manufactured, not naturally established.

The more they dug into this direction, to more they were reassured that art and literature are key. Yet their influence could still not reach as far as it could. They concluded that this basic 'nutrition' was feeding the minds of a few fellows. The circle needed to be bigger.

"The bigger the circle, the better,"

they thought, for the fruits of their cooperation.

"This needs a vision of a world in which innovative entrepreneurial and social enterprise solutions will be used to alleviate poverty in a feeling of mutuality,"

they agreed.

Focused, they tried to learn more about art and literature, especially about how the methods and materials, used to educate artists, changed considerably over time.

Throughout early periods, most young artists received their early training as apprentices. However, much later, learning about art theory gradually became as important as mastering practical skills. By the age of industrialization, art had evolved from a craft to a course of academic study.

They decided to learn more into fine art and fairy tales because of a clear interest in multidisciplinary arts and crosscutting areas and issues. Issues such as responsive and flexible support to talented and visionary friends to develop their personal vision and drive, giving them the chance to make their mark as part of a vibrant arts ecology.

Ever since there were limited opportunities. These missing opportunities throughout communities impeded fellows to access the support that is needed to turn bold ideas to achieve social change into a reality. Particularly fellows operating outside of an established organizational context faced adversities.

ARTS AND LITERATURE

A stronger education system, including the encouragement of entrepreneurial thinking, was vital to the development of the creative and skilled minds that will generate the future economy. However, the need for literature to create independent, critical, alienated subjects was far beyond fully satisfied: Could they develop opportunities for more general fellows who want to progress ideas that they believe will lead to positive change?

Readers wanted literature to be politically engaged, to tell the stories, such as the struggles of oppressed groups. So collectively, they decided that they could cooperatively provide real support through skills training, access to networks, communication, and advocacy.

"Through peer-learning and collaboration we can better understand how to combine culture and arts with other societal issues, supporting the valuable crossover between the cultural sector and other sectors,"

they proposed.

"What was more exciting than building the bridges between the generations to make sure that culture is both an asset to be enjoyed in the now and a legacy to be appreciated in the future?"

"Culture matters. It always has, and it always will, in a civil society, "

they concluded.

THE DARKEST MOMENT

Just so close to a world in peace, authoritarianism and populism were once again looming to overrule politics for the first time since long years.

Faith in democratic institutions was shaken. It has brought to the fore dangerous forces that many fellows never even knew existed.

Suddenly, the world had another shock wave. A pandemic outbreak made everyone stay distant from their fellows to avoid deadly transmission of a virus that changed the world order overnight. Large communities came to a standstill.

Everybody around the world was put under lockdown. Living together gained a different meaning for all. The sudden break of life brought this time major problems for people on every continent. No one was spared. Bitter recriminations and panic represented more than just fear of the future, they reflected a basic confusion about what was happening and the historical story that brought everyone to this moment.

Yet everyone knew that in the long run the firms that would survive will had to master a challenging environment as the crisis and the response to it accelerated one mega- trend: an energizing adoption of new thinking to counterbalance a worrying rise in

WELL-CONNECTED GIANT AUTOCRATIC

POWER GROUPS.

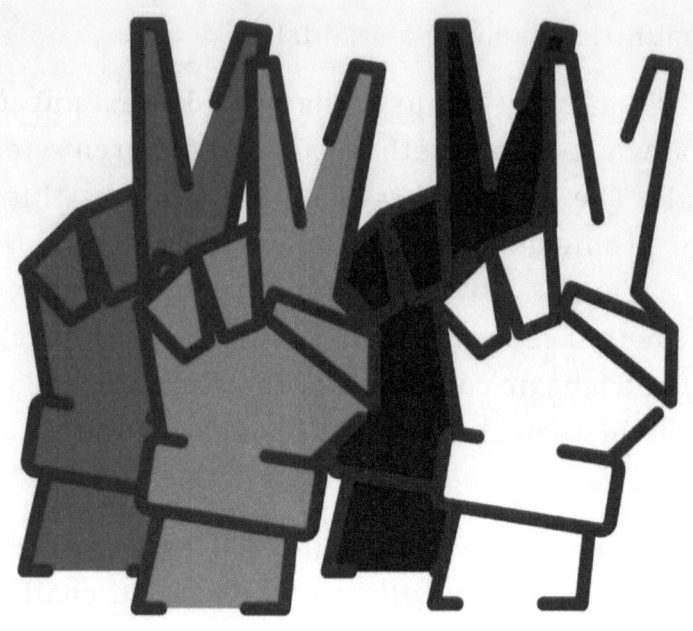

Xapuri, Brazil 20h33,
21 December 1988,

Strong beliefs in green self-determination and empowerment can be dangerous. For years before his murder, he had received death threats. Though, he was not an easy target to kill. Having tried to kill him in half a dozen unsuccessful attempts before, no one knew that better than his enemies.

However, in the months before his death, some men observed him this time from a square near his house. On the evening of December 22, as he stepped just two feet away from the door outside of his wood-frame house, while the two policemen who were supposed to protect him were playing dominoes at his kitchen table, he became the target of bullets fired towards him. He came back in the house, walked about a few yards, and fell down near his bedroom door. His wife tried to lift him, but he fell down again. This time, he was not lucky to escape.

The bullets were shot exactly a week after his 44th birthday when he had predicted he would "not live until Christmas". The assassins triumphed the end of a man who had won global acclaim for championing the sanctity of the forest. He had organized resistance in the form of human chains that blocked developers' incursions into the forests. The threat that would persist for indigenous people and for the environmental balance of our planet had finally overcome a milestone barrier -known as Chico to everyone - and his mindful reminder that in another fifteen years or so, little of the rain forest may be left to be saved.

His murderers were arrested and found guilty and were sentenced.

Yet the attack was just one in a series of assaults that already had claimed more than eight hundred lives and was going to claim one hundred more lives since December 22, as over the last half-century, one-fifth of the Brazilian Amazon disappeared as a result of deliberate action: man-set fires, mining and relentless bulldozing.

When Chico was dead, it was a terrible feeling. It was very sad. At that time no one was concerned about the forest. At that time poor people defended the forest.

"My dream is to see, to see this entire forest conserved because we know it can guarantee the future of all the people who live in it."

Quite unthinkable at the moment when he was assassinated, yet, Chico's early death became a turning point in international environmental consciousness.

Everyone started asking questions.

What was going on?

In Brazil, and other countries, some were talking about social, ethnic, economic, and geographical 'apartheid' as well as grim inequalities as the root of the problem.

"We must ensure that solidarity, which was expressed at the time of the funeral, attended by some thousands of mourners, remains as strong as ever." everybody shouted.

They had realized that what at first was looking like a fight to save trees, was a fight for humanity.

From then on, nothing would ever be as before!

But after a while, human beings started to forget day by day. They went – back to business - as usual as they restarted to sing

"Mamma Mia, here I go again!".

4

THE MASTER

STATISTICALLY speaking, it is very unlikely to have a sincere conversation with someone who is shot at the head. Even the chance is not zero, in such a real scenario, please do not expect the victim to come up with - what you would think as *likely* - as an answer to the question

"How does it feel like to shoot in your head and not die?"

"The bullet went through my right side first, then through me, and out my left side. Unbelievably

I did not feel anything. Yet, almost instantly I was soaking wet with blood. By the sound of the bullet entering and exiting I realized that I survived.

Despite having been the victim of the bullet!

I couldn't hear out of my right ear. Immediately, I felt an extremely hot burning on my right side. To be precise: the bullet entered my right temporal region and came out of my right eye socket. As a result, I lost my right eyeball, and my right orbital floor was smashed. Now I have a metallic plate as my artificial cheekbone. Ohh, do you see, this big bone above your eye, which I say my eyebrow bone, was also kaput. In 7 different places. Along with a few others in my ear and those around my right temporal area as well as my eye socket, a result of a total of 34 breaks in the surrounding bones.

Two years later I still remember the moment, when my blood had already started making a small puddle on the floor; and I am still amazed about how I did not feel the bullet entering and exiting my head. As I have already repeated so many times answering when I regained consciousness at the hospital to everyone who has asked what happened:

It was a **MIRACLE!**

But if these amazing things were not happening now and then, what kind of other life would be nice?

I am still just amazed by the whole incident in general but especially how I did not feel it. I cannot explain it nor could the doctors. As unbelievable the story is, I assure you, it is all very true, unfortunately.

The lack of pain did change though. After I gained consciousness 7 days later, I soon realized the extent of my injury and how the pain was most definitely present then. Two years later there is still pain.

So, my answer to the question of what it feels like to get a bullet in the head:

"It would be like getting hit in your head with a sledgehammer and if you can still think, your head must be still at least attached, right?"

***

NEW life order under confinement was calling everyone for the deepest insight in history:

"The spirit requires no new matter or energy besides that of its organ, but only order and harmony in the matter or energy at hand!"

In simple words, it meant that new thinking was required with our hearts and souls. To see with our hearts and soul that the reason we are on Earth is to form the human family, existing together because we were made for one another."

For all of us, striving to be better in the future means doing something right now and starting this from somewhere near our homes, even from our own garden. The important thing is that we can create a more beautiful garden in terms of solidarity and harmony within our environment. We must internalize this solidarity; However, the foundations of our future solidarity will be built on a different understanding that depends on our seeing the world with our hearts. Not a kind of solidarity, where the powerless being at the mercy, the powerful supports him from a higher ground, but in mutual respect and understanding that personal well-being is unconditionally dependent on the well-being of the other.

For a moment, he thought of Jack and their story of mutual fascination, friendship and love, starting from that first conversation to the centuries beyond, in the company of two people who tried to stay apart but found out that they couldn't.

Now in the network age, those with long lives have acquired a rich repository of experiences that they can use to help guide others. Elders thus represent the source of wisdom that exists in each of all fellows, helping them to avoid the mistakes of the past, while reaping the benefits of life's lessons.

Social ecology deserved a hearing as an appeal not only for moral regeneration but also, and above all, for social reconstruction along ecological lines.

Yet, the jury was still trying to find out if this latest phase could be called an improvement. The battle was still not decided against the ecological abuses that communities had inflicted on the natural world by going to the structural as well as the subjective sources of notions like the 'domination of nature'.

'Jacques, The Master' decided to use the new networks as platforms to actively contribute to a version of the future he wants to live in.

The times of pandemic and confinement was therefore suitable to divert full attention into the physical, mental and emotional health. Somehow, he had to try to challenge the entire system of domination engraved in words. In minds. In almost everyone. He went on to reach minds that would easily allow questions to be raised. Questions to seek to eliminate the hierarchical and class edifice that has imposed itself on humanity and defined the relationship between non-human and human nature.

DIE TRYING

New latest generation networks were in the process to unleash the greatest technological shifts in a generation, one that promises to instantly deliver speeds many thousands time faster than current best mobile devices.

Indeed, experts were since some time predicting that this new technology would eventually replace almost every internet connection on earth.

Being a slow-thinking, slow-moving man now, he was resisting the world of speed. He routinely did not know how to express something valuable he has seen along the way precisely to afterwards feel about it, until he sat down and wrote about it. This was partly because so far, he had been walking for too long; through the beauty of the landscape, the headiness of mountain passes and the sweetness of forest trails.

Now under confinement, he obviously had less motion. To avoid feeling like a dead leaf, his voice was permanently stressing the need for embodying ethics of complementarity in social institutions, providing active meaning to its goal of wholeness, and of human involvement as conscious and moral agents in the interaction of species.

He remembered that Jack once told him:

"Most of us already know that it is very crucial to write your mind down. The simple act of writing makes things visible and tangible. But there is one rule you need to follow to succeed: It is not enough to write things down; you must describe them in complete detail!"

In tranquil tiredness, writing became for him like a flame inside his heart. He experienced extending himself inwardly in introspective activities, and outwardly through concerns about the welfare of others.

He could write about many topics:

political tyranny, concentration of powers, autocracy and dangers to individual liberty and democracy, faith in democratic institutions, environmental and financial collapse, space exploration etc.

In any case, he knew that allegory was his only way out.

He decided to use it as a literary device to express large, complex ideas in an approachable manner. This way he could help them create some distance between themselves and the issues they are discussing, especially when those issues are strong critiques of political or societal realities. Like a simple story that represents a larger point about community or human nature, whose different characters may represent real-life figures.

Sometimes, situations in a story may echo stories from history or modern-day life, without ever explicitly stating this connection. For example, exploring the difference between approaching life as a game with an end, or a game that goes on forever. How to better express the idea playing to win is not nearly as satisfying as playing to keep the game going?

Yet, he did not know in which genre he was supposed to write. He thought fairy tales contain substantial constants that actually provoke and facilitate a literary self-conscious stance.

Was that his favorite genre?

Yet, it was considered as an underdog genre. Most authors with a literary theory and debate chose it for meta-fictional play, or formal experimentation.

He was not sure where and how to start. After all, there was information overloading everywhere. He remembered Jack mentioning:

"Your writing isn't an accident. You were meant to write. You are filled with gifts, those gifts aren't just for you, even though you can and should enjoy them. The gift we possess is meant to be shared with others: Your stories are not just for you. They are for readers who need something. Perhaps your readers need to be encouraged. Perhaps they need to be thrilled or simply not to forget things that they loved and embraced long time ago. No matter your genre or style, your readers come to you out of a need that they can't meet anywhere else. Think about it, this way: When a reader chooses a story, it is because that story is satisfying a hunger within."

'Jacop, the Master' took pen and paper but before putting the first sentence down:

ART AND LITERATURE TOWARDS A WE-CULTURE

A fear rushed him out of the blue: He was afraid that the world he would create in his writing would be less friendly and alive than the world he used to live in.

Jack advised him:

"Are you paralyzed with fear? That's a good sign. Like self-doubt, fear is an indicator. Fear tells us what we have to do. So do not be afraid, do not write either a fiction, or a non-fiction but something rather new, something else that you think is good enough as a need for something life itself rarely offers. It's a taste, perhaps, of what life is supposed to be, but can't be for so many tragic reasons."

Listening to Jack's advice, 'Jacop, the Master' decided to do something new, creating a taste for a kind of mix between fiction and non-fiction, where nature is involved in a vision of all being as essentially alive; a sense of profound inner freedom and liberation, may be more than a perception of universal love or compassion extending to all beings, a paradoxical sense of standing beyond and encompassing flow of particular events etc. Particular events!

Such as the dance of the bees in a hive, working for the good of the group. Yes, most importantly particular events, such as the cultivation of an affiliation with the interests of the community, one, in which the communal interest was placed above personal interest, or, more properly, in which the personal interest was in par with and realized through the common.

Under confinement 'The Age of Exhibition' was over. What became more important now was communication.

How could he help communicate through art and literature to as many people as possible?

At the end art influences society by changing opinions, instilling values and translating experiences across space and time. So, he decided that he should write about art and literature as tools of communication; to allow people from different cultures and different times to communicate.

To communicate with each other via images and stories.

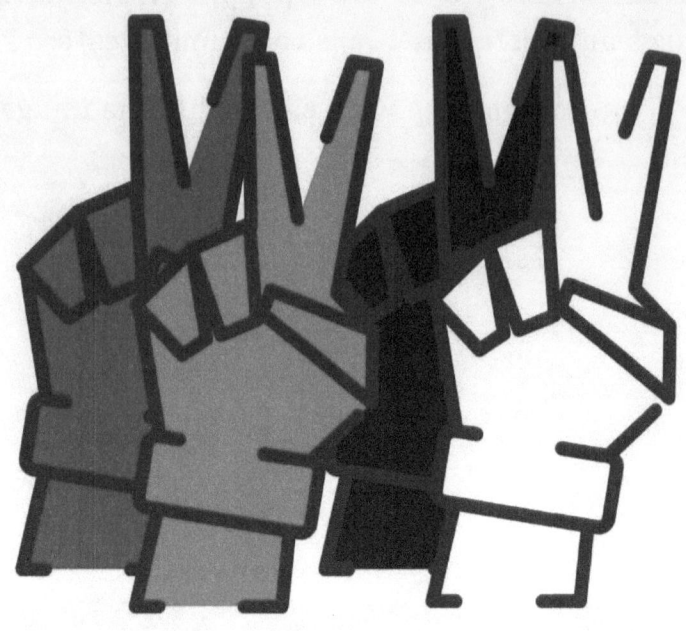

Around the Globe, 20h33,
01 February 1973,

Strong beliefs in purple self-determination and empowerment can be dangerous.

The lower the average age of the population, and the lower the development pace of their origins, enslaving the youth in poverty, it is more likely that the youth can find any ideas that seem liberating very alluring. Especially, when a young assassin and a young victim are not educated about the other, the results can be deadly.

For years before her murder, she had received death threats. Though, she was not an easy target to kill. Having raised two children, she was tied to life like a coin to a magnet. Having tried to kill her in unsuccessful attempts before, no one knew that better than her husband.

However, in the months before her death, something changed dramatically. She entered a world dominated by men in a country where women's political participation was rapidly growing. They were fighting together for women's social, economic, and political achievements. Yet, despite her and her friend's sustained efforts to deal with discrimination and violence against women to call for gender equality, they failed on February 2.

One day before the shooting, when she had entered the assembly, there were shouts of

'Get out!!!;'

when she wanted to speak, they did not allow her. Ultimately, she had to leave the assembly to protect her physical integrity, because the manifestation was quite scary.

Dropping her children to her friends after school, on this evening of February 2, she arrived home, anticipating that something awkward was going to happen.

As she stepped into her bedroom and took a seat at her dressing chair, she was frightened as she faced her assassin in the mirror who was dressed casually. Completely naked, she became the target of a single bullet fired towards her head. This time, she was not lucky to escape.

The neighbors who were shocked by the sound of the gunfire called the police. By the time the ambulance took her to the hospital near her home, it was 21:30. To the surprise of her doctor, she did not die. The police could not find out where the assassin was hiding.

Seven days after, when she woke up from a coma, it became clear that she had been receiving threats from her husband ever since she got married. When intimate partner violence was too unbearable, she would ask for help from her friends, who would often pay more attention to the violence instead of how helpless and hopeless that violence makes her feel. Yet, nobody in her friend's circle realized that she may have felt the only way out is to kill herself; this time it was not her husband. The casually dressed assassin and the naked victim were the same people.

Tragically, her attempt was just one incident in a series of assaults that already had claimed more than millions of lives and was going to claim millions of more lives since February 2, as over the last century, one billion women —one out of three women around the world—faced and would face intimate partner violence or sexual violence in her lifetime.

Yet, her unexpected survival became a turning point in international women's consciousness. Everyone started asking questions.

What was going on?

In Canada, some were talking about poverty, historic marginalization, racism, and legacies of colonialism as the root of the problem, making women frequent targets of hatred and violence.

Soon also other countries have realized that this is a genuine risk of harm to both perpetrators and their victims and what at first was looking like a fight to save women, was a fight for humanity.

The 10th September was declared as Suicide Prevention Day worldwide.

"Despite progress, one person still dies every fourty seconds seconds from suicide," said World Health Organisation Director-General, many years after the funeral.

"Every death is a tragedy for family, friends and colleagues. Yet suicides are preventable. We call on all countries to incorporate proven suicide prevention strategies into national health and education programs in a sustainable way."

On World Suicide Prevention Day, the World Health Organization launched a "Fourty seconds of action" campaign to raise awareness of the scale of suicide around the world and the role that each of us can play to help prevent it.

From then on, nothing would ever be as before!

But after a while, human beings started to forget day by day. They went – back to business - as usual as they restarted to sing

"Mamma Mia, here I go again!"

5

THE MASTERPIECE

TEMPORALLY TRYING to bypass the perceptions of his past, but losing control now and then, he collected his material before he started to type.

He had found the essence of his twenty-five thousand manuscripts in five thousand pieces of paper with very fine writing. Then he had read what he had written and decided that the information on these five thousand papers could also be summarized.

Then he started writing as if painting a canvas with his words. As he banged away, he – like the greatest of the great dreamers - watched them take shape like magic before his eyes: Now he wrote the summary of these five thousand papers in only one hundred-page thin book.

As soon as he finished the summary, he understood that he was tired. He felt that the end was approaching like any other.

After all, he had been through, he was afraid that others would have his books and manuscripts, so he had thrown all the written documents into the ocean except that one thin book.

Now he had nothing but a book with a summary of all the wisdom in it.

THE BOOK

ART & LITERATURE

TOWARDS A WE-CULTURE

By
THE OLD-FASHIONED
MASTER

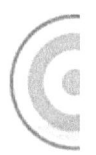

Uniting the Reader
with an Author and an Architect
to Discuss

3 Sculptures / 3 Narratives
on
Life/Death/Life cycle
and
its power on unified consciousness

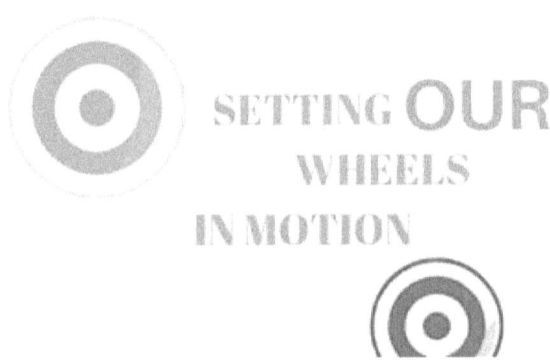

SETTING OUR
WHEELS
IN MOTION

Original Title:

ART AND LITERATURE TOWARDS A WE-CULTURE

Subtitle:

Uniting the Reader with an Author and an Architect

To Discuss 3 Sculptures / 3 Narratives

on

Life-Death-Life cycle and its power on unified consciousness

Norsk utgave © 2020

H. Aschehoug & Co. (W. Nygaard), Oslo www.aschehoug.no
Tilrettelagt for eBok av Type-it AS, Oslo 2020

ISBN : 979-XX-51-60782-2

ACKNOWLEDGMENTS

I am grateful for some great friends in encouraging me to start the work, preserve with it and finally, share it. I would like to say thank you to Jacqueline, Jack and his grandparents, and everyone who shaped, shapes, or will shape his thoughts on stone or paper.

FOREWORD

ART AND LITERATURE TOWARDS A WE-CULTURE unfolds rich intercultural myths, fairy tales, and stories, interpreting 3 different sculptures, to give a humble example that can help us reconnect with ourselves and others, not necessarily when only things go wrong, because we all are strong until we become vulnerable.

Through the stories and commentaries around these sculptures, we retrieve, examine, love, and understand the Brakes of Life and hold it against our conscious but also subconscious world, both at the same time. These marvellous fairy tales originated from a wide variety of little tales thousands of years ago that were widespread throughout the continents. Today they continue to exist in unique ways, yet under different environmental conditions.

Under the shower of the narratives in this book, our subjectivity will take a walk through the fertile and life-giving sources in our soul – to let go what does not work for our well-being. In other words, it will take a wellness bath through the stories and commentaries relating to those selected sculptures. This non-verbal communication will visually occur through the reader's observations on the work of the artist in such a way that they will inspire the fierce, healthy, visionary attributes of our instinctual nature.

What becomes genuine through the reader's participation is his choice to eventually join other readers in an online virtual visit of the architect studios where all participants within their schedule, including the author, they will create a symbolic ritual to have a structured conversation about the role of art and literature toward creating a We-Culture .

Using Your Code

ART AND LITERATURE TOWARDS A WE-CULTURE aims at a new mentality in its call for a collective effort to use art and literature for the support of National Health Services, in each country around the World.

Using the Zoom Meeting Code*, provided by this specific book, the idea lies first in creating a loop between three parties: an architect, an author and the reader, who is the observer but most significantly a self-interpreter with desires: The reader will thus have a chance to volunteer in participating to a free session and can provide questions that will be answered during each week's 30 minutes Studio-Visit-Webinar. While we are exemplifying how we can use these fields, which serve as a compass, in our daily lives, and how to be careful about the fact that art and literature can unwittingly or consciously hunt us down. It puts the reader at the helm so as not to be knocked over in dangerous bends, and reactivates and regains it back to the society when it hangs in the life-death-life cycle.

We-Culture, including an architect

The selection of the architect has not been arbitrary but rather a natural outcome of many subsequent events and features: When the author was temporarily working abroad, under confinement in Montenegro, he had a unique chance to visit Art Basel online for the first time as the institution made all its galleries accessible for everyone during four days. While enjoying various works of art, the author realized how important it is that art can be accessible. After a short research, it revealed that a Canadian entrepreneur took this idea and developed a platform to make art accessible to broader circles than only galleries, and therefore their limited circle of clients.

Contacting her opened one subject to the other and this is how the author learned about a book (1955), Plagued By the Fire, on Lloyd Wright who is not just the greatest of all American architects, but who during his career overcame different breaks of life until he finally became a global name influencing others, especially creating an educative environment to foster a WE-CULTURE, embodying his bedrock principle of "an architecture from within.

"Not only the aspect of naturalism and minimalism but also, among others, understanding the Life-Death-Life cycle," finds Damla SEVIL, a young architect, who -thanks to her international experiences on the job- was interested in psychology, especially for the awakening of her consciousness. She brilliantly communicates the importance to find peace, balance, and harmony as a whole, a hand-shake so to say between technology and art, or science and psychology.

SEVIL is reluctant to interpret the abstract sculptures, exhibited in this book. 'Every person who observes the piece is going to look at it from their perspective, or own life experiences.' she says from her studio in South Muğla.

"That's most exciting because then the work becomes interactive; it lets people wonder why it is there in the first place." She describes her perception of artwork as 'an intersection of art and literature.' It is not hard to find precedents in history for Damla's interest in both science and art.

THE LOST ART OF SELECTING THOUGHTS

A valuable package has just arrived. It is a new book. It's short and the title writes:

Welcome to the World of
Conceptual
Art

A TRIBUTE TO
THE IMPORTANCE OF SELECTING THOUGHTS
TO PROTECT
OUR BEST INTERESTS

'Beethoven's Trumpet (with ear), opus 13',
John BALDESSARI
2007

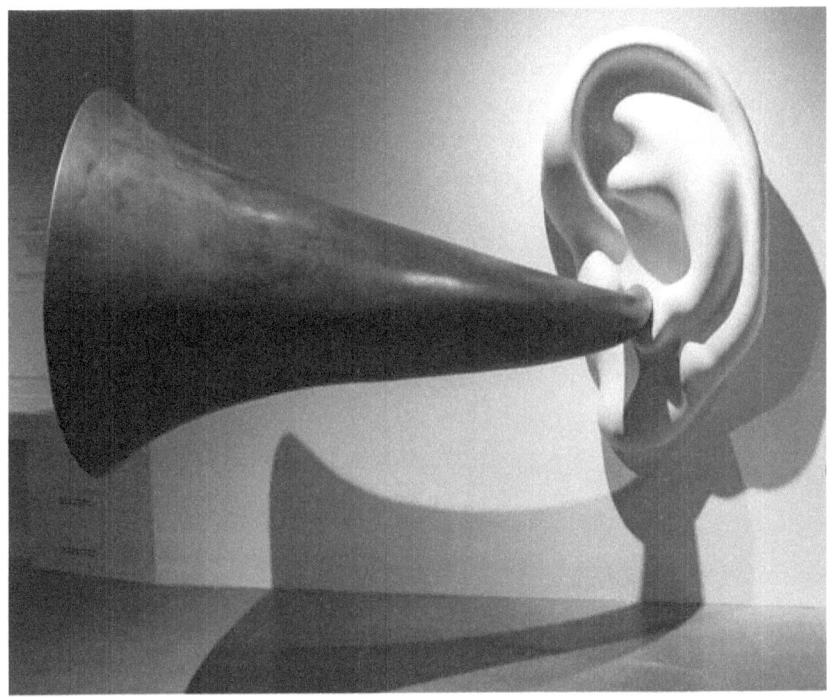

This April 23, World Book Day was being celebrated by millions of people and over 100 countries in lockdown. Launched in 1995 by UNESCO, World Book Day celebrates the joys of reading and the authors who have shaped our world. With schools closed and families at home, books are more important than ever to generously stimulate minds and inspire hope.

Being a generation in unprecedented transition, today we are open to new ideas and are tolerant of 'the others.'

When asked about the engine of these tolerance wheels, one thing comes to mind right away: Curiosity is our essence in the genetics of human intelligence, naturally presented to us like an ore. When artists and writers awaken our curiosity, they can change our minds for a lifetime.

It is intrinsic to human intelligence to be curious in any kind of language framework. Time and again, artists and writers transit through different languages. Through art and literature, a generation can search for their freedom, express themselves in very peaceful and creative ways in inclusiveness, now much better than older generations.

But before going into attempting to understand something nearly impossible as conceptual art, let us have a look, how back then other concepts were used to stimulate minds and inspire hope.

The oldest form of literature describing life here and there have been oral stories.

The Conversation,
Monad BALKAN
1994

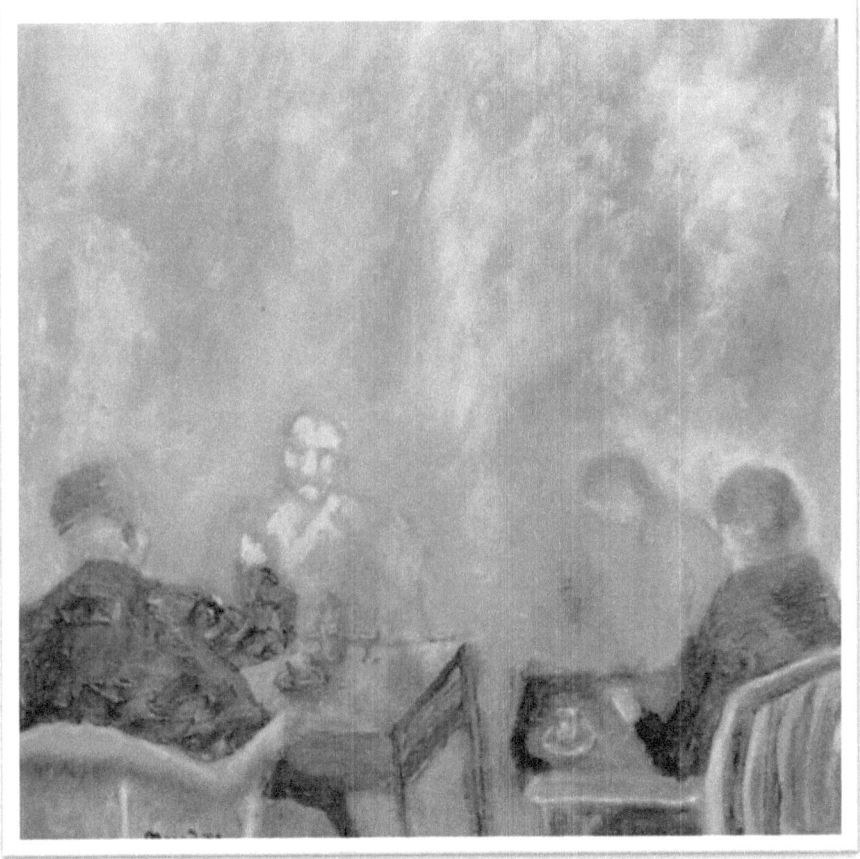

Image: Courtesy of the Artist

Children learn these stories from their parents, who learned them from theirs and this goes on from generation to generation, like water takes the shape of the hose it goes through. We relate these stories to our friends and even sometimes we use them to make them our stories.

As fairy tales have become a general part in the civilizing of the West – all from Charles Perrault from 1697s to the Walt Disney cinematic fairy tale of today's culture industry – many of our ancestors and even today, presumably many of us living in so many different cultures, have been embracing them as a set of standard, being disposed to them, but not being necessarily aware of its perilous side!

The enchanting features of fairy tales can disarm, take us off-guard sometimes; especially if they are used to discreetly shape our consciousness and sub-consciousness for an end. Throughout centuries this indoctrination aimed mostly to conform generations with certain social codes. Although our connectedness can blind us to other moral concerns, our common experiences are often among the most cherished of our lives. Our bee-like nature facilitates not only altruism or heroism but genocide and war, too. Consequently, understanding the power of unified consciousness, and questioning the intention of its originators is important.

The Little Prince,
Antoine DE SAINT EXUPERY
1943

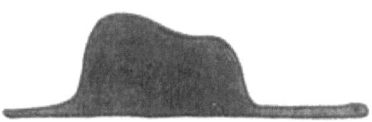

I showed my masterpiece to the grown-ups and asked them if my drawing frightened them.

They answered: 'Why should anyone be frightened by a hat?' My drawing did not represent a hat. It was supposed to be a boa constrictor digesting an elephant. So I made another drawing of the inside of the boa constrictor to enable the grown-ups to understand. They always need explanations. My drawing No. 2 looked like this:

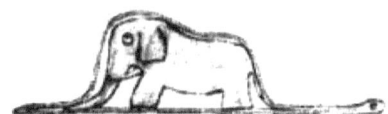

Although the true origin of *The Little Prince* is widely debated, many suggest that Saint-Exupéry was inspired by this Hans Christian Andersen fairy tale. In the early 1940s, Saint-Exupéry was stuck in a hospital while he recovered from various injuries that had piled up from his plane crashes, and he was bored out of his mind. His friend Annabella decided to read him a story—"The Little Mermaid"—that got Saint-Exupéry thinking about writing a fairy tale of his own.

What is the meaning of fairy tale within the evolution of Culture? Fairy Tale signifies belief in the supernatural, not the suspension of belief. We all believe in the extra-ordinary of Once Upon a Time because we want and need to believe.
Yet the question remains: What can be so **dangerous** about fairy tales?

The relationship of fairy tales as art for subversion is analyzed in great detail by Jack Zipes 'Fairy Tales and The Art of Subversion'. He warns us against the objective of molding our inner lives by 'high art' which can be all but harmless to the reader and thus becomes contradictory. Confusion can cause self-limiting and self-distracting beliefs. And if our intelligence – in our body, our cells, our nature – is working against us, instead of working for us, as it should; well…how to tackle this problem?

Abstract Art And Not So Innocent Fairy Tales

What do we think of when we imagine a fairy?

The first image that likely jumps to mind is of a diminutive, winged entity – sometimes taking the form of a perfect woman – who uses her magical pixie dust to perform benevolence for human beings. While this wholesome representation of fairies commonly populates children's storybooks in modern times, they have a darker and more sinister folkloric past.

Some old stories from England, Ireland, and Scotland, for example, portray these supernatural fairies as wicked, soulless, and temperamental that were not above murder, if you landed on their **bad side**. They are not always tiny, either. Depending on the region, they can be the size of a human, or even bigger.

Hereafter the reader will rely heavily on impartial judgment when reading through the stories and commentaries to associate this book's narratives to be filtered by only one goal: entertaining communication without exploiting our 'innocence'. This means that the narratives will avoid using enchantment for a higher-end, to reinforce social codes or to discreetly mold our inner worlds, without the purpose to like or dislike certain elements of an artwork, or other constituent parts in or around our social configuration.

When people get together to talk about literature or art even life in general, do they find common ground and compromise?

Do we consider all perspectives? In short: **No!**

We all are different. And we all think differently. When groups discuss an issue, members might take extreme positions they are inclined in the direction of their pre-dispositions. So how should we approach abstract art after all?

And why shall we care at all?

To answer these and other questions, let us examine its key focus on one of the most common and perpetual patterns in everyone's own life.

THE BREAKS OF LIFE.

And who knows? By the end of it, we might all change our minds.

When All Doors Are Closed

For Hemingway, one of the greatest writers of all time, it was war, love, and death that triggered a reaction in his inner world towards the breaks of life. He came to a deep understanding of its far-reaching implications. For Frank Lloyd Wright, one of the greatest of all-American architects, it was a crazed servant burning down his house in Taliesin, Wisconsin, and murdering or fatally wounding seven people, one of whom was the woman Wright deeply loved and had been living with. For me, it was the destruction of my native village.

Similarly, when The Breaks of Life hit us, we have a feeling of a big loss. For so many of us, such a loss is inconsolable. Yet, the way we will look at things after a healthy period of mourning can change the way we feel about them.

If stories and comments help us discover newer perspectives on our subjectivity, or encourage meeting other people, this will be to help anyone to experience the reconciliations, wonders, or joys, which have once become one's own.

"What we have once enjoyed deeply, we can never lose. All that we love deeply becomes a part of us," said Helen **Keller**, who had met the Break of Life from its harsh side – at her birth! She was the first deaf-blind person to earn a Bachelor of Arts degree in 1920s US, influencing our world as an author, political activist, and lecturer.

In opposite to death, life means new. New people, ideas, and a different way of looking and thinking can be effective. And when it seems that all doors are closed, a window can open. Conceptual Art helps us get familiar with finding unexpected views and looking at new perspectives:

When we relate to choices made by an artist or a writer, we may redefine what we want from life, feel better about ourselves, find the good enough balance between chaos and perfection in the wilderness of each of our inner 'cities'. As Zipes put it: 'to breathe life into our daily undertakings.' Such breathing life, on the other side, is an everyday task of a public space artwork.

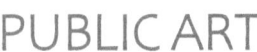

PUBLIC ART

Public Art is not a new phenomenon, as everyone admires the impressive sculptures created in the Hellenistic period – today's Greece and Turkey provide almost an open-air museum in these regards - yet it has been an important part of American public spaces only since the 1960s when the 'National Endowment for the Arts' established their first public art program in America's public spaces. During this inception, public art was a new concept in a time when art was largely relegated to the confines of the museum.

Ever since the notion of public sculptures enhancing the public space started to capture people's attention, they drew meanings from the contents of the space around them, especially if such air was filled with freedom.

Interestingly, public space art has been a popular outcome in cultures, where democratic roots flourished compared to those who suffered or still suffer under autocratic regimes. A sculpture can make people think and thinking can be a dangerous act because a different way of looking and thinking can be effective! Exactly this effect is dangerous for conformists, when some content of conceptual art brings to surface topics or part of it, which does not match the expectations of its observer and catch him off guard. It may feel a bit out of the blue to the person who receives it. That's okay. It's good. If Contemporary Art can catch us off guard with a signal that someone cares, and that someone is thinking about you:

100 years ago, when an eye disease forced a talented artist in France at his 40s to give up tapestry weaving, he turned his full attention to sculpture – luckily for us. However, the French

sculptor, painter, and printmaker Aristide Maillol's monumental statues of female nudes created a big concern for the general public.

Some societies around the World today still argue that the nude form is something that should be hidden away in the artist's classroom. According to how radical they look at things, such people often attempt to stop others from viewing or learning from the human body.

"What spirit is so empty and blind, that it cannot recognize the fact that the foot is nobler than the shoe, and skin more beautiful than the garment with which it is clothed?" would answer Leonardo **Michelangelo**, an Italian sculptor, painter, architect, and poet who influenced Western Art much longer ago.

Yet Maillol rejected the highly emotional sculpture of his contemporary Auguste **Rodin**, preferring to preserve and purify the sculptural tradition of Classical Greece and Rome. His major works show the emotional restraint, clear composition, and serene surfaces Maillol employed in his sculpture for the rest of his life. He wanted to remove literary and psychological references from his sculptures; the resulting generalized figures emphasize form itself. With the use of mainly natural elements in his sculptures, he not only expresses ideas of naturalism but also attaches prudence in his communication through visual ways, in accord with those concerns of Jack Zipes about fairy tales.

L'air,
Aristide MAILLOL
1938

Paris Jardin Tuileries, Lead

50h x 94w x 36d in. (130h x 240w x 93.3d cm)

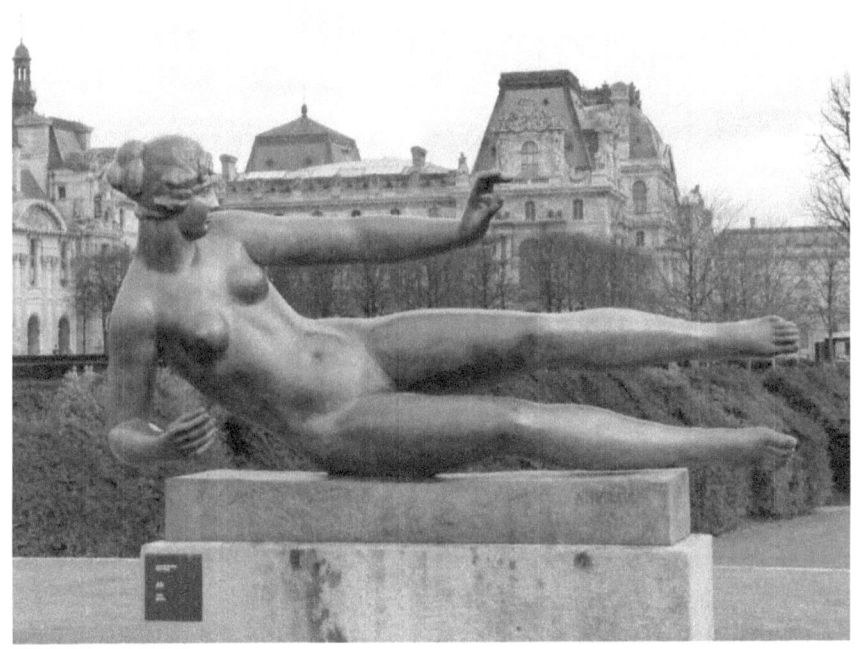

Therefore, it is less surprising that the choice of the artists in this book will favor on one side abstract sculptors, offering this book room for the attachment of psychological and emotional elements that Maillol kept his fingers from, but on the other side sculptors who are or have been active in a cultural environment or society that is mostly open to new ideas.

Though Maillol's connection to the art of the past was strong, his interest in form and geometry helped to pave the way for abstract sculptors such as Constantin Brancusi and Jean Arp to Maya Lin, whose work will be accompanying the stories below. Surely, art and literature yield a powerful form through which both individual and societal values can be transformed. Stories tell us about ideas, which can sometimes be difficult to deal with.

It is interesting to find out that oral stories have been widely available throughout many, many generations, for example in the Caribbean region, while the written form has only been a recent phenomenon: written folktales have been available after the 1960s when many Caribbean nations were freed from British rule. This indicates that throughout the world, from Africa to the Caribbean, both the redirection of politics and recuperation of the oral culture is at the core of modern writing with the hope to bring us closer to whom we are and how we process this notion of being.

Despite many break downs, *how* did Wright processed this notion of being?

We would never have heard about his bedrock principle of "an architecture from within" if he had not built his own astonishing Guggenheim Museum on Fifth Avenue, still the strangest building in Manhattan, many years after the murder of the women he deeply loved.

Perspective view of the
Solomon R. Guggenheim Museum in pink © The Frank Lloyd
Wright Foundation Archives/The Museum of Modern Art/Avery
Architectural & Fine Arts Library, Columbia University, New York
City/Artists Rights Society, New York City.

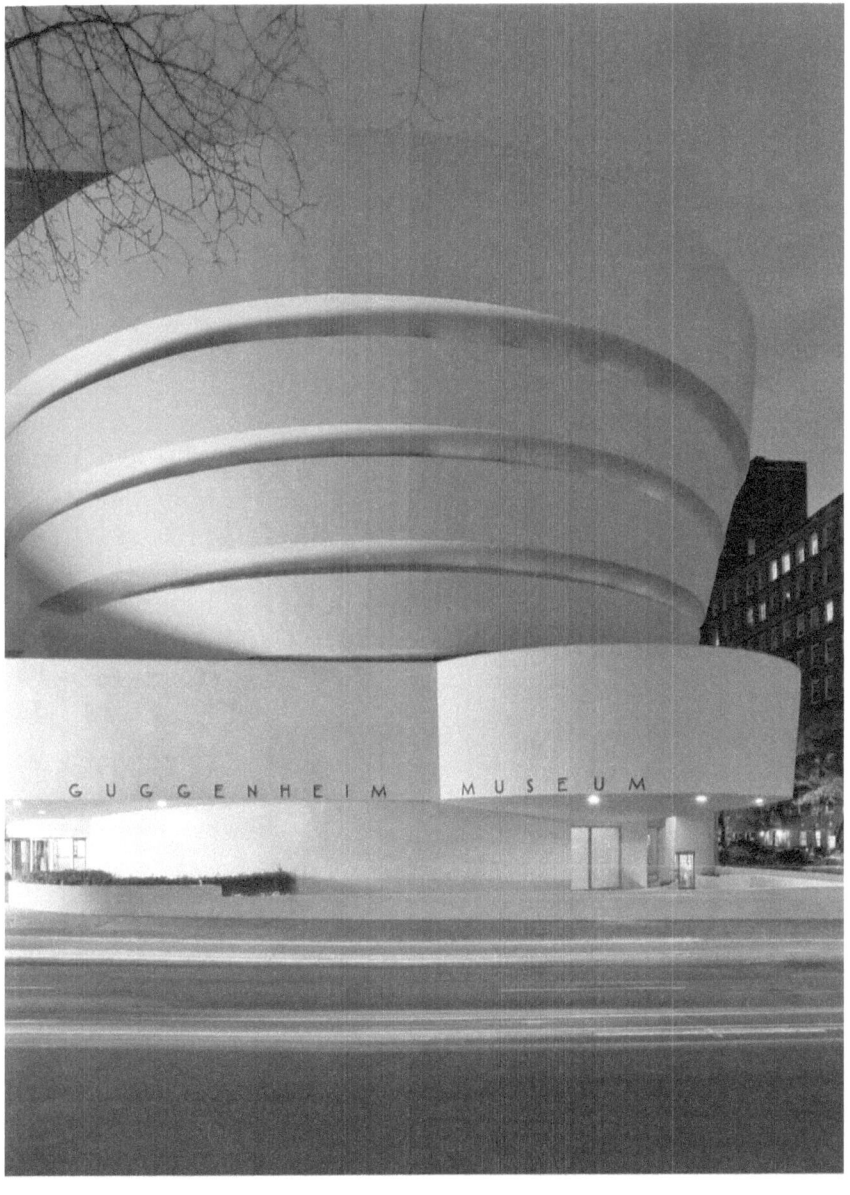

In other words, both the sculptures and the narratives in the coming sections mirror each other, opening an honest and sincere communication with the reader, without any afterthought, but with a fineness, that praises peace, spirituality, independence, yet connectedness. In such a world it is easier to find a system of inquiry capable of achieving what Contemporary Art or Literature does:

Passion and suffering can open our eyes and sharpen the powers of observation. Yet the only word of any sustainable value is the written.

So, let's use it, right here, in this book, to move us closer and closer to truths that improve our lives and understanding of the universe. In the end, Nature has only been able to evolve us so far and no further. To evolve to our highest potential – being freed from a division of the mind such as race, color, sex, social class, etc.-, we have to take evolution into our own hands and learn to enjoy our self-driven trajectory. Freeing ourselves from the blinkers and blind spots that beset many of us, we can harness a critical new ingredient: cognitive diversity. Our reinvention will bring extraordinary benefits to break free of the echo chambers in our minds. Because when we sing a song, we are expressing our whole soul. And when our heart is filled with full of love and goodwill, we radiate peace. Like Conceptual Art, radiating ideas as the song of

JUBILANT SOUL.

THE BREAKS OF LIFE

ONCE UPON A TIME

Once upon a time there was an orphan girl without shoes. But she collected all the pieces of fabric she found and after a while she sewed a pair of red shoes. Their appearance was coarse, but she loved them. Even though the days passed by gathering food in thorny woods until the weather got dark, the shoes made her feel rich.

One day, as she walked down the road in rags and with her red shoes, a sudden gilded carriage stood beside her. There was an old woman in it. She said I would take her home and act like her own little girl. So, they went to the house of the old wealthy woman. The child's hair was washed and combed. She was given clean white underwear, a beautiful woolen dress, white stockings, and shiny black shoes. When the girl asked about her old clothes, especially her red shoes, the old woman said that her clothes were very dirty and her shoes were so ridiculous, so she put them on fire and burned them where they became **ash**.

THE BREAKS OF LIFE

When things occur unexpectedly or that we do not think of as part of the ordinary cycles of life and nature, they arouse strong emotions. They force a new realization about how we can approach and understand the complexity of human suffering.

Arthur **Miller** (1915-2005), a famous American playwright had a firm grasp of the tragic dimension in each of us and strongly advocated that attention must be paid. This comprehension of The Breaks of Life can be visible if we look at an artwork for a long time and with **serious focus**.

A great example is Pablo **Picasso's** Guernica, about the horrors of war, in Madrid.

The coronavirus pandemic provides a recent example of negative forces with deep impact tied to rapid consequences proved us once again that we as humans are endangered species. But is there something inherently good to discover about it, if we were to change our minds how to look at it?

The girl in the fairy tale was very upset because the simple red shoes she made with her own hands, despite all the wealth around her, gave her the greatest happiness. Now, in the house of the old woman, she always had to sit well, behave as told, and not talk to her without permission; so, a secret fire began to burn in her heart, and she continued to miss her old red shoes more than anything else.

It is highly understandable to ask why there are such brutal episodes in fairy tales. This phenomenon is found in myths and folklore around the world. The creepy end of this tale is typical for fairy tale endings, where the spiritual hero cannot complete a transformation that begins.

Surprisingly, many of Barnett Newman's sculptures look as if a giant has come at it with an axe and hacked a piece off. It's gorgeous, unpredictable, vulnerable and deeply alive in contrast to the rusty planes that barely seem to contain it. All massive pieces have something broken and fragile in Barnett Newman's sculptures: his pursuit of the sublime lay less in nature than in culture.

"A house that does not have one worn, comfy chair in it is soulless." a prolific Belgian-American poet, novelist and memoirist, May **Sarton** imply.

The breaks in *Broken Obelisk*, perhaps the best American sculpture of its time, can be beautiful, like the internal life we all struggle with and have to embrace.

Broken Obelisk,
Barnett NEWMAN
1967

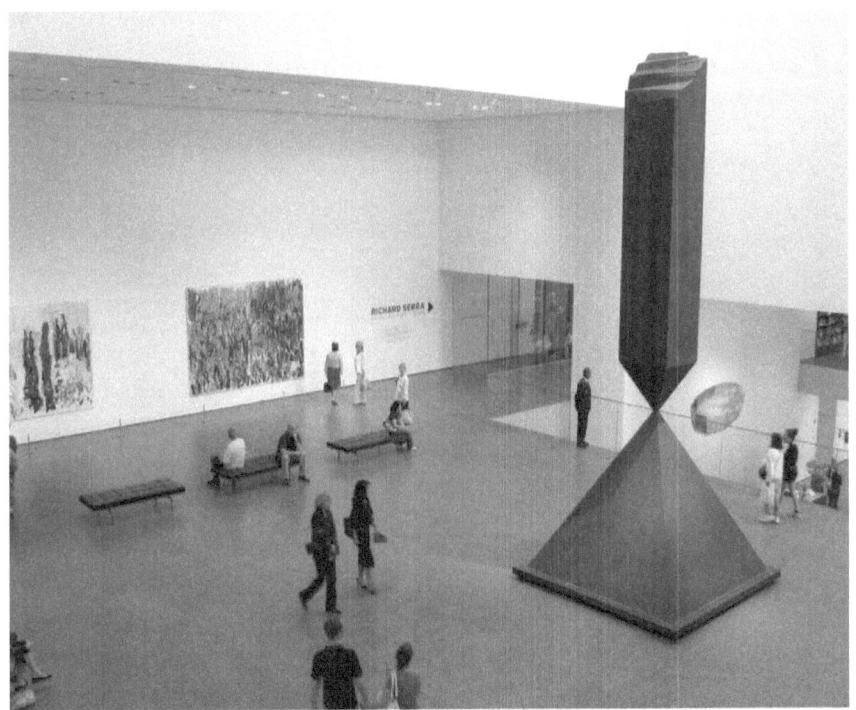

CorTen stainless steel
Image: The Museum of Modern Art, MOMA, New York.

How does the story evolve? Will the girl be capable of effective change this time or is she doomed to be a prisoner of her red shoes dancing her around and around?

If emotions control our acts, then thinking can guide our emotions.

As her red shoes makes her dance, she enters the cottage of the oldest person in her village:
"I think last time you wanted to tell me that there was a reason why our civilization acted weird. You told me that you will reveal me a secret,"
she asked.
"Yes"
said the oldest man and added:
"Life is like school, kid. Like in school there are some people really enjoy inflicting pain to others. They do all sorts of things. Some very violent actions but also some not so violent, still inflicting suffering to others. This makes them feel good. They get a satisfaction from their behavior.

Yet take the pleasure out, there is nothing more behind this, only chaos behind a seemingly perfect exterior. In real life this behavior can also be seen in economic relationships, when some people try to outsmart the society, by extracting common resources and so inflicting pain to others – without providing an added value to their community but funnily – or not so funnily – outsmarting themselves at the end. What we call economy is a conceptual system of a reflection of the society and the individual's culture of thought and a reflection of the social organization. When we look at the people who do these selfish, greedy actions, we can see that they are economically very rich, but there is nothing in their lives other than money. The economic motivation of people who live their lives in this way can be so strong that they can tolerate the killing of innocent people who are contrary to 'interest'.

Yet take the profit out, there is nothing more behind this. Their motives and the color of their bullets - unlike the different colors white, black, green, or purple attached to their victim's visions - are always the same.

What I find interesting is that over time, the once haughty man - divided the universe - has learned to shed his egoistical exterior, and works toward improving his life and those around him. He can take earnest interest in the lives of those in his community, for example comes to the aid of a homeless child, or benevolence activities in general. He can learn to embrace life and inspire others to fall in love with his example uplifting others."

When living in Pera, Constantinopolis around 1920s, and witnessing the sema ceremony of the Whirling Dervishes **George Ivanovich Gurdjieff**, an Armenian mystic philosopher said:

"Man lives his life in sleep, and in sleep he dies," asserting that people in their typical state function as unconscious automatons, but that a person can 'wake up' and become a different sort of human being altogether.

Fire is a good companion for our mind.

Surely, on one side there are barriers set by our environment or innate self-distracting forces leading us to delineate from our true inner passion. We sometimes move away from people, we want neither to belong nor to make an effort, but keep apart. We sometimes feel we have not much in common with them, they do not understand us somehow. We build up a world of our own, all the trappings of our own design. Then all we do is with nature, with red shoes, with books, or dreams for eternal dispute.

But on the other, we intuitively know that no matter how bad the situation we might be stuck in, we are capable of creating Positive Powers that magically can come to shine to transform ourselves, as subjective self-interpreting beings with desires. Within each of us there lives such a powerful force, filled with good instincts and compassionate solidarity driven from ageless knowing. Most of the times conflicts cannot be resolved by rational decision. Surprisingly they can be resolved by changing the conditions within our inner world that brought them into being. The subconscious mind controls most of our lives, and only a small rest is run by the conscious mind. Hence most people live life on autopilot mode: Once habits have been ingrained into the mind, they are just repeated day in and day out unconsciously. But we have a choice to go from auto-pilot to decision maker. The decision will be ours to remain asleep and unaware or we can wake up and come to the realization that we have the power to live life in whatever way we want to live it. Naturally, and even strangely, this change can even be inspired through simple things, for example through listening to birds in a forest.

Our **attitude** is critical to gain unlimited access to our minds.

Newman's sculpture was not designed for a particular site, and it commemorates no specific person. Some interpret *Broken Obelisk* as a universal monument to all humanity. The steel pyramid, from whose apex an inverted obelisk rises like a beam of light. Here, did Newman want to bypass the western associations of pyramids and broken columns with death, and produced a life-affirming image of transcendence?

Even before the coronavirus pandemic our species long past was strained with full of events that suddenly and unexpectedly broke lives. Back then, if those were lucky enough to survive, ended up somehow to find themselves in a situation of urgency, a need for adaptation.

Broken Obelisk is abstract work. Even though the emblematic power of the materials from which it is constructed and the context of the historical environment in which they were made are important, they are often kept out of the conversations. Yet highlighting their meaning can be effective to counteract an erasure of their socio-political content.

Does *Broken Obelisk* hint at the social unrest of the Civil Rights Movement and Vietnam War protests occurring in the United States in the 1960s and urges **a new way of thinking**?

Not only but surely during this pandemic we witness an unprecedented amount of solidarity, a new way of thinking, organizing, and mobilizing of resources and most of all a powerful embracing feeling that we all depend on the well-being of each other, no matter how far we might be, ideologically, physically or financially.

Even it is less surprising that coronavirus pandemic has put on hold many key moments in the fundraising calendar, including marathons and other sporting events, we witness an unprecedented way of transformation. For example, the 99-year-old World War II veteran **Captain Tom Moore** wanted to raise funds for National Health Service (NHS) Charities Together, a UK-based charity supporting the work of the National Health Service, by walking 100 laps of his 25 meters long garden before his 100th birthday. He quickly broke through his original target of £1,000 ($1,200), and thanks to media coverage has now raised more than £26 million with donations from more than a hundred thousand people.

Life works in mysterious ways:

What may initially feel like breaking can sometimes transform into

BREAKTHROUGH!

OUR INNER CITIES

CREATING A LOOP

This book aims to follow 100 years old Captain Tom Moore's footprints for a similar kind of collaboration, this time through the use of art and literature for the support of National Health Services, not only in the UK, but in each country around the world, basically by local readers.

The idea lies first in creating a loop between **three parties**: a sculptor, an author and the reader, who is the observer but most significantly a self-interpreter with desires:

"I know about my consciousness through my person of view."

This has a private nature. Yet this privacy can come with a cost. It can make life difficult to connect and get connected.

Our brains consume much more of our body energy even though it is composed of only a few of our mass and seems like a universe within. We are far from understanding of how it works, yet some argue that our built-in curiosity is a good source to look outside of ourselves and eventually find a re-connection.

Many of us reading these words right now, may be facing struggles. Perhaps because of dealing with addictions, harmful relationships, or negative thought patterns that have led to hopelessness or depression. We may be overwhelmed by fears or desires. We may want our fears to go away, or we may wish our desires will be fulfilled. In either case, these emotions lead to suffering.

After she had listened to the oldest man in the village, time and weeks passed and nothing seemed to change or improve! She kept dancing in her beautiful red shoes. When she grew tired of this routine and feared that she will never be able to escape her fate, she became angry and started to cry.

In Newman's pyramid these rusty, oxidized hunks of metal have "tears" — meticulously hand-polished surfaces that symbolize "breaks of life, division, neglect, forgetting". These tears can cause **an illusion**.

So, can we come closer to understand in a unified consciousness – now more than ever – how we can act as a part of the whole, despite all possible setbacks and our own personal limitations bound to time and space around us?
Hans Christian **Andersen's** famous story tells of a little bird born in a barnyard who suffers abuse from the others around him until, much to his delight and to the surprise of others, he matures into a beautiful swan, the most beautiful bird of all. This story is beloved around the world as a tale about personal transformation for the better.

In 1999, Jerry **Pinkney** adapted the story as a children's picture book. In 2009, the Dance Theatre of Bradenton, Florida, presented the ballet version of the popular tale *The Ugly Duckling*. In 2010, **Garri Bardin** directed a feature-length stop-motion musical of the story set to Tchaikovsky's ballet music. And in 2012, a musical adaptation of the story, with ten original songs, was released by JJ's Tunes & Tales. The album, titled "The Ugly Duckling: Story with Songs" contains both songs and spoken narration, and was released independently on CD Baby and iTunes.

The binding problem, *how* our brain integrates different information it gets into our conscious and subconscious experience, is what makes us all **unique**. In real life the brain is terribly good and puts everything together; the movement, the shape and the colors for instance. Science wants to explain a big part of this puzzle, yet after a long history creating and understanding art and literature, we believe that witnessing the wonders of nature, art and literature, has its own way of healing.

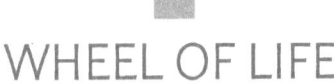

WHEEL OF LIFE

The subconscious is a concept developed by Sigmund Freud in his theory of psychoanalysis. According to this; Consciousness structure is another structure that works in a much deeper and invisible region behind the states of consciousness that are seen. The subconscious is complex; It is blended with both biological hereditary instincts of primitive sexuality and aggression, as well as compressed memories, thoughts, desires and impulses.

Since the subconscious elements push the individual to a constant unrest, they cannot directly come into consciousness. For this reason, only sometimes it manifests itself. According to Freud, experiences, emotions and thoughts that are pushed into the subconscious can also occur with dreams and dreams. Freud himself also used the data of his subconscious in explaining human behavior.

For another thirty-one-year-old young but prominent psychoanalyst Carl Jung, Freud was not only a respected colleague, but a father figure from which he could open his heart and mind. According to Freud, Jung was energetic and an exciting new candidate for psychoanalytic action. But this strong bond between them has changed throughout their friendship. What were their stories?

Stories and post-traumas were unprocessed, hidden in myths.

In 1970s a Jungian psychoanalyst, **Clarissa Pinkola Estes** started to work on this topic. In her book published more than 20 years later in 'Women Who Run with the Wolves: Myths and Stories of the Wild Woman Archetype' she wrote:

"Sometimes the one who is running from the Life-Death-Life nature insists on thinking of love as a boon only. Yet love in its fullest form is a series of deaths and rebirths. We let go of one phase, one aspect of love, and enter another. Passion dies and is brought back. Pain is chased away and surfaces another time. To love means to embrace and at the same time to withstand many endings, and many many beginnings- all in the same relationship."

The more we were stuck at one step of the Life-Death-Life nature and the more this problem made headlines, books paid more and more attention to it. These days the bookshelves almost of each bookstore are filled with books of inner transformation. Yet, the ever-increasing products on this same subject creates an information overload in the time of corporate consumerism, leaving us behind a feeling of being exploited rather than helped, thus arousing a feeling of being exposed to them, if not being disposed.

If someone looking for remedy through them finds luckily a good-enough narrative to truly enjoy a sincere communication to inspire one genuinely, then yes, the reader opens up. A good book is like a **good friend**.

"We have to dare to be ourselves, however frightening or strange that self may prove to be." would our friend May Sarton share.

The truth is that a good friend is way more influential to condition our minds, bodies, and emotions to link pleasure to whatever we choose.

"I think of the trees and how simply they let go, let fall the riches of a season, how without grief (it seems) they can let go and go deep into their roots for renewal and sleep.... Imitate the trees."

By changing what we link pain and pleasure to, we can sustainably change our behaviors. With excessive drinking, for example, all we have to do is link enough pain to drinking and adequate pleasure to quit drinking. We can have our questions answered. We can feel, think and then act to gather and collect our soul back to itself.

Can we see our own world through a different lens, that someone else has a different view point than of our **own**?

After the anger stage subsided, the girl took off her red shoes. Eventually she came to understand and accept her lot in life and this way learned how to enjoy it. The next day, she was mysteriously freed from the endless time loop.

Wheel of Life,
Gustav VIGELAND
1940

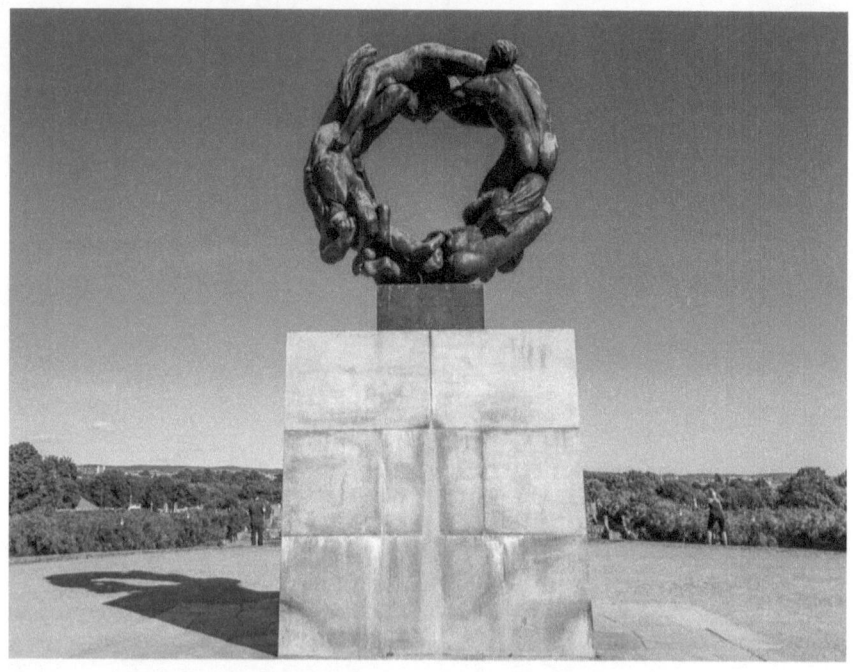

The Vigeland Sculpture Park is the world's largest sculpture park made by a single artist. The Norwegian artist Gustav Vigeland dedicated his life creating it, working on this project from 1924 until his death in 1943.

The Wheel of Life is a sundial positioned at the very end of an eight hundred fifty-meter axis. Thematically, it continues the journey-of-life motive prevalent in the rest of the Sculpture Park. It represents eternity, with four human figures and a baby locked in a circle, floating in harmony. Does this harmony imply the successful transformation from the wilderness in-between Life-Death-Life cycles? Miraculously this harmony extorts its power to tackle our inner barriers, those self-distracting beliefs yielding to isolation and seeing the world as chaos and perfection only.

As any traveler knows, travel changes you in ways you never could have imagined. And the next best thing to experiencing it yourself in a dream destination is to take a virtual journey inside an exhibition, travel movie or well-crafted fairy tale. That's where the very best books about travel and self-discovery come in. They make perfect gifts for travelers. There are many books written about self-discovery, listening to your heart, and following your dreams such as *Zen and The Art of Happiness* or *The Alchemist*. Many including famous and successful people recommend reading them. As with good books, it takes not once but more times reading to truly enjoy because only then we find in ourselves what was not there before! A response comes from our subconscious reflecting the nature of our thought we hold in our conscious mind. We embark on a journey to become what we think about. Is this not the most striking thing that makes us HUMAN?

THE CONNECTEDNESS

US, AND ALL THAT AROUND US - AN ILLUSION?

Artificial intelligence, so popular these days is great deal of explaining objective tasks but are doomed to remain outside the door of the hard problem of explaining of how we get subjective experience from our brains. Picasso once said:

''Art does not depend on the use of a beauty canon, but on the instinct and the brain to imagine beyond any canon. When we love a woman, we do not start measuring her limbs. We love with our desire - even if everything is done to use a canon, even on love.''

Nevertheless, in the effort to find meaning, our quest for measurement went on with more rigor than ever before. Complex problems demand that social scientists collaborate with others. In the roll call of potential collaborators, natural scientists loom large. Better measurement to predict in more precise ways.

The law of attraction, or simply call it the **'love' relationship** between matter and energy was seen not very different from those in our own romantic lives. It is full of mystery, fueling its dynamics on and on. Trying to understand its deep implications, obviously causes headache for many, but especially for scientists who wanted to come with a mathematical solution.

Starting from **Isaac Newton**, after a long search over centuries basically until recently, in just two years, 1925 and 1926, scientists developed the idea of Quantum Mechanics. There were initially two versions, one formulated by **Werner Heisenberg** and one by

Erwin Schrödinger. Surprisingly, those two turned out to be equivalent.

Like for so many misleading directions in science before, until that time, starting with the belief that our world is flat, by 1925 everyone believed that basically they are physic laws that rule all things that are of matter. If we were able to see these rules through observations, laws of quantum mechanics with the naked eye, it would surprise us then, as these laws do not follow the laws of perception that we attribute to understanding what is happening around us, in form. In fact, quantum physics proves that atoms are made of energy and are not actually tangible matter.

WAVES OF HARMONY

Such illusion happened to mankind ever since the first consciousness arrived. What Newton held in his hand on an atomic level did not even exist—it was an illusion. Newton's so-called reality can be called in our modern time an illusion because an illusion that is something that is seen—however—is **not real**. And this is thanks to the development of Quantum Physics.

But back then life was different. In the old Latin quarter in Paris stands a magnificent 18th century building—the temple to all the gods, the Pantheon. Originally constructed as a church dedicated to St. Genevieve, it was later converted into a mausoleum containing the remains of famous French citizens such as **Voltaire, Jean Jacques Rousseau, Victor Hugo, Emile Zola, Marie** and **Pierre Curie**, and **Jean Moulin**.

Today, the Pantheon resembles less of a church and more of a museum. The church had long been stripped off its altar. In the apse, instead, hangs from under the central dome, a large metal pendulum that challenges the very beliefs the Church once held.

In 1851, a 32-year-old Frenchman, a drop-out of medical school diverted to photography, definitively demonstrated that the Earth was not flat but indeed rotated, at the shock of the French scientific establishment. His elegant scientific demonstration has been delighting us for nearly two centuries to come:

Léon **Foucault** had determined that he could use a pendulum to illustrate the effect of the Earth's movement, when called together a group of scientists, enticing them with a note declaring,

"You are invited to see **the Earth turn**."

Foucault hung a pendulum from the ceiling of the Meridian Room of the Paris Observatory. As the pendulum swept through the air, it traced a pattern that effectively proved the world was spinning about an axis.

What the Foucault experiment meant for the scientists to come after him, the double-slit experiment was this time for quantum physicists. It has similarly become popular. A classic thought experience, for its clarity in expressing the central puzzles of quantum mechanics. This popularity comes from its power to demonstrate the fundamental limitation of our ability as the observer to predict experimental results. **Richard Feynman**, an American theoretical physicist, who was awarded the Nobel Prize in 1963, called it 'a phenomenon which is impossible to explain in any classical way, and which has in it the heart of quantum mechanics. In reality, it contains the only mystery of quantum mechanics.'

Since we are all made of matter, quantum physics allows us a glimpse into how this plays our illusion of reality. What we perceive does not actually exist—it is not our true reality. Quantum physics proves this by winking an eye suggesting it can be less paradoxical to spirituality than previously assumed.
Water Line (2006) reflects this by its fluidity. In *Water Line*, Maya LIN, an American sculptor positions the viewer at the bottom of the Atlantic Ocean, or, more precisely, beneath the bottom of the sea floor and raises questions about space, substance, systems, sensation, but most strikingly what our

'true'

reality

can be. Can you see a dolphin family dancing around in circles?
They were swimming just there a minute ago.

Water Line,
MAYA LIN
2006

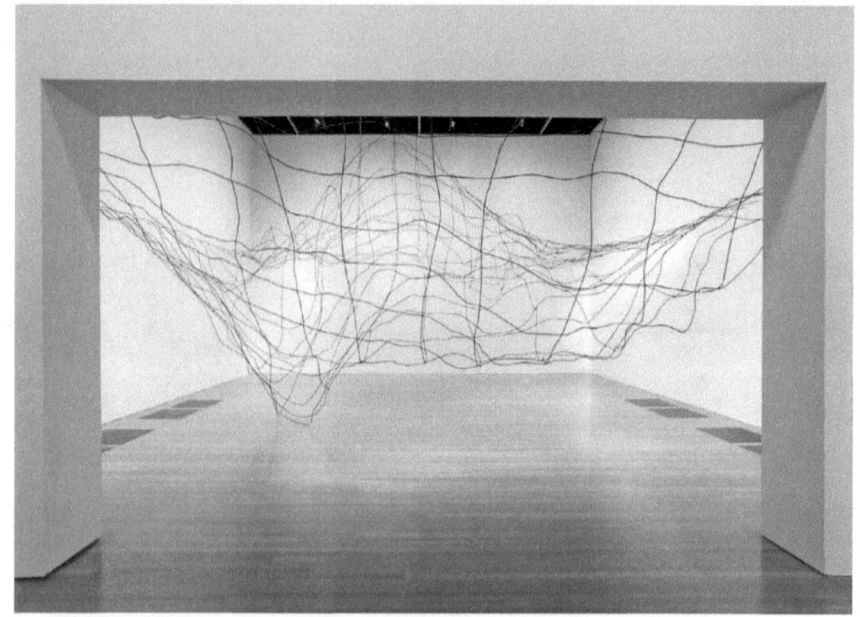

Installation view, *Maya Lin: Systematic Landscapes*, de Young Museum, San
Francisco, October 25, 2008–January 18, 2009.

Courtesy of the Fine Arts Museums of San Francisco.

"My affinity has always been toward sculpting the earth." Maya underlines.

Are thus particles of energy which build our spirituality? And is it because of our energies proven ability to influence, it is indeed conscious? If so, how can art and literature help to bridge the cultural time lag **between divided minds**?

The twentieth century, of course, was the century of disciplinary specialization. Yet social science has not always been cast in such a subsidiary role in science and technology. Lin's impulse was little remarked upon at the beginning of her career when she was known mostly as a creator of urban commemorative sculptures, the first and most famous being her Vietnam Veterans Memorial for the Mall in Washington. Designed when she was still a graduate student in architecture at Yale, this long, black granite sculpture inscribed with names of the war dead was as much a monument to healing and humility as to heroics, and it became a flashpoint for American feelings about a divisive war and a disorienting era. Yet today, when we hear some loud voices in Washington, somehow still alluring for some TV channels, it seems there is still room for maneuver for such a healing.

The act of seeking to understand is a controversial one because it requires a degree of empathy with the 'freedom firebugs' that kill the peace within all of us, including women, environmentalists, pro-democracy spirits, blacks of African origin and the elderly in general. Everyday attacks – be it economical, physical or ideological, all around our planet have complicated attempts to understand freedom firebugs because the act of empathy can easily be confused with outright sympathy for murderous attacks. However, one cannot get into the mind of freedom firebugs to discover the layered or interwoven meanings of their -mostly to themselves unfamiliar- sacrifice without immersing oneself in their grievances, religious rhetoric, and symbolic universe.

Understanding and explaining are not necessarily opposed methodological positions, although their research requirements can differ significantly. To explain freedom firebugs, at least as they relate to why individuals become 'human mosquitos', we need to first understand the social meaning given to these acts of extreme violence by their perpetrators. Thus, we must, first and foremost, seek to understand the symbolism of self-damage and sacrifice. The staging of questions is an unmistakable response to the stunning — and, to many, alarming, situation in our modern times which evolved over nearly a decade and was a response to some countries succumbing to varieties of odious political domination, isn't an explicit knockoff of a single party, ideology or leader. Its real target is any citizenry that rather lazily does not or cannot respond.

THE LAYERS OF MEANING AND HUMAN CONNECTIVITY

Like waves, having **mood swings** are just normal reactions to the ups and downs of life that everybody experiences. Think of a gigantic whale soaring through the ocean, swallowing each and every fish of any size that moves across its path, or a dolphin family dancing around in circles.

Is it our automatic dysfunctional thinking that perpetuates our depression?

If so, this can keep us in a downwards spiral of negative thoughts about ourselves and the world around us. With mindful guidance, we might learn that these negative thoughts are not reality. Rather, they are dysfunctional beliefs about ourselves and our life, and are something that can be replaced with more realistic and healthier ways of thinking.

We do not know the answer for sure, yet a work of art or literature is best placed to raise such questions. Recalling the famous dictum over the Platonic academy in Ancient Athens Lin gravitates toward the formal purity underlying Modernism. At the same time, however, she often manipulates visual form of the water to unveil successive layers of meaning.
Nevertheless, social and scientific disciplines co-exist and occasionally they are obliged to interact. Many of us observe, especially through last couple of decades, a periodic engagement and disengagement of these disciplines, and the emergence of a formalized rhetoric of interdisciplinarity, as **an antidote** to disciplinary specialization.

However, works of art or literature are the best platform to address such questions if the purpose of its creator is to progress in the path of social positive values, such as sincerely supporting the reader or his observer, lifting him or her to his feet. The role of art is to ask them in the first place rather than answering the questions and to generate interest and curiosity in the observer who watches the works with interest.

The "know yourself" doctrine, which was first introduced by the Spartan Khilon, took place at the Temple of Apollo in Delfi and has affected many thinkers significantly.

The thinker Plato in ancient Athens has succeeded in expanding the ring for the wisdom of the society, and conveyed his view on the academy to the benefit of everyone from the erosion of time, still worth sharing with us.

Today's art reminds us to remember this, for example, by sculptor Lin, this time by drawing our attention to the purity underlying modernism.

Water Line (2006) embodies waves in an ordinary room. On the one side, it makes large amounts of water visible, imaginary vast oceans. Watching an ocean, our attention may be arrested by the soaring flight of a fish, or the bolting leap of a wave, or the low-slung shadowy loping of the shimmers. Yet the physical, chemical and biological processes are heavily intertwined in these waters. What we are really witnessing in such cases are the mere kinetics of physical motion, caught in the frame of an essentially static image of the scene before our eyes. It can deceive us into believing in the 'eternality' of a single moment in nature.

In fact, the ocean suggests the Life-Death-Life cycle: It comes on waves, ebbing and flowing. Sometimes it is calm and other times it is overwhelming. We can **learn** how to swim in it by thinking and questioning or reading, by seeing in ourselves what was not there before!

The old man continued:

"When I dig below the surface, I realize that these people are open for a powerful message. A message that needs to portray them the evolution of a main character from self-absorbed and cynical with an appetite for destruction to selfless and optimistic. Without a role model or a good example in their lives, people, given the opportunity to repeat his day over and over again, choose to act selfish and careless to others. But in the end, mostly after exhausting his options that hurt himself and others, man can choose to use his life to love himself and those around him.

Life is like school, kid. If we perform exceptionally well in our courses, we go on to graduate. But if we fail, we have to repeat our classes again. At this point, we can awaken from our 'hypnotic sleep' and mysteriously free ourselves from the endless time loop. Yet the strange secret is:
We cannot change the world; we can only change **ourselves**!"

Similarly, oceans bring up the topic of waves into the surface that Einstein used to call 'gravitational waves', a notion, that as the Double-Slit-Experiment shows, opens the doors for understanding our cosmos.

Gravitational waves are disturbances in the curvature of spacetime, generated by accelerated masses, that propagate as waves outward from their source at the speed of light. They were proposed by **Henri POINCARE** in 1905 and subsequently predicted in 1916 by **Albert EINSTEIN** on the basis of his general theory of relativity, using beautiful mathematical equations, in which even Newton's equation of gravity fitted perfectly.

Interestingly, Lin's installation *Water Line* (2006) provides us a visual expression to the archetypal devolution **from unity to duality and then to multiplicity**. Scientists love this idea of the Big Bang. Bearing almost universal associations with creation and its progressive differentiation, -the famous **marriage between evolution and entropy**, in the words of **Brian GREENE**, a famous quantum physicist and the founder of World Science Festival "a primeval reality containing within itself the germs of a multiplicity of beginnings and beings."

Wave Line (2006) is a strange and wonderful combination of the intelligible and the sensible but requires viewers to imagine themselves small in order to transport themselves into these constructed worlds. Only then we can sense many intelligible layers potentially contained within unity. Like the apple Newton saw falling, consisting of both matter and waves at the very same time.

WE NEVER STOP LEARNING

Like waves, feeling **sad** is a normal reaction to the ups and downs of life that we all experience.

As often heartbreaking life can be, we all secretly know, that exactly there lies its beauty. The dice are already thrown; everything has an end, not only our lives but also our planet, our sun and even the whole galaxy, one day in very far future. That future, far for some, and not so far for others, depends on the way we look at things. Do you think this is a depressing perspective?

May be not! Let's try to approach the subject differently together!

For long time scientists, even Albert Einstein doubted the existence of black holes...the 'accelerators' of momentum for gravity, the master entertainers in our cosmos, without which there would be no light-show, to put it playfully. This changed when evidence came by the new generation after Einstein, which – thanks to the progress in technology- could observe and thus prove their existence, even the one in our own galaxy.

Dikkat, tehlike! Bu bir kara delik değildir.
(Be Careful! This is not a black hole.)
CEM TANRIÖVER
2020

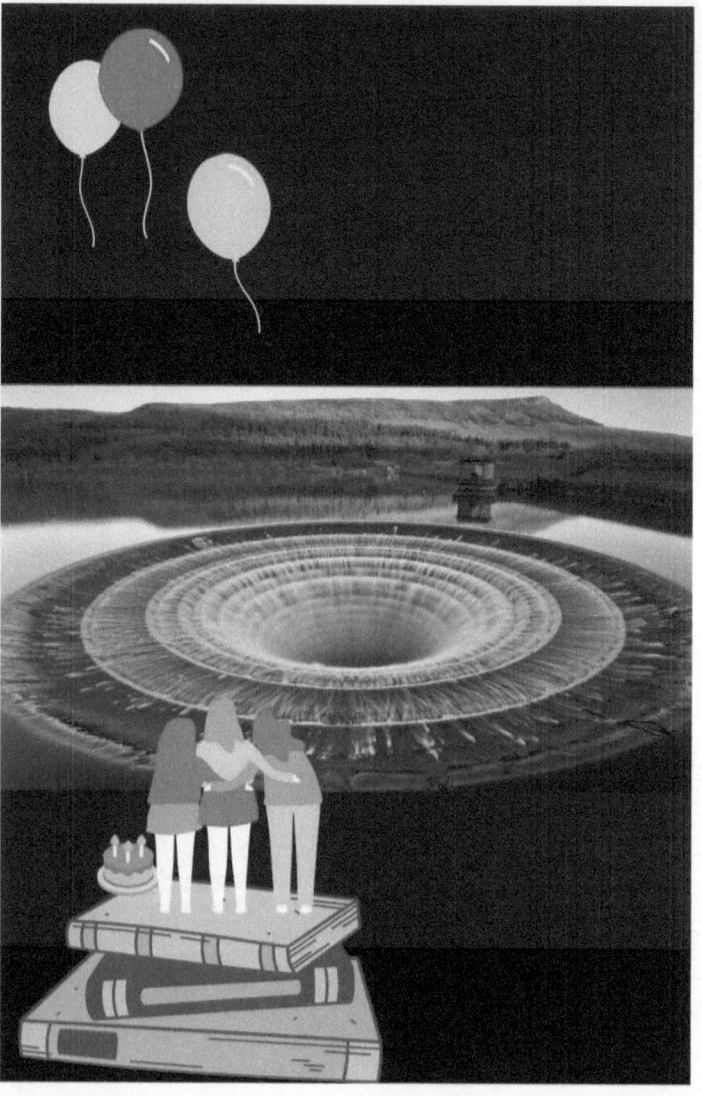

621,9 km away from Heinaut, Belgium; Derbyshire Reservoir

Now, the "grown-ups" discouraged the Berkshire Reservoir from being a black hole because they could not see beyond the simplicity of the drawing to the true creativity that lived (or perhaps, more accurately, no longer lived!) inside. Ah, the grown-ups...

Mr. Brian Greene shares during each years' Science Festival nice images of two such black holes linked to each other creating a new form, the so-called wormhole, as the point of interest to analyze if time travel is possible.

When two black holes unite, the process of connection ends when a newly completed form, a wormhole becomes finally visible. In some sense it looks like a kiss of these two black holes. A wormhole? Ahh, what a name for such a beautiful kiss!

Like when we kiss, wormholes offer us the best short-cut for a journey into the complex universe. Time travel is a short-cut because some it can connect distant corners of the universe, even different universes, theoretically so that a traveler does not have to go all the way to get to its destination physically. Foolish head weary feet?

Putting down our feet on the ground, coming back to Earth from space, we see those wormholes right here every day. They become visible each day on the streets, frankly everywhere. Love. We look around and all we see is love.

Yet, it only occurs in a sustained way when two people can deeply connect. They open their way to the destination and listen through the channel, with an ever-changing effect where thoughts and emotions and everything travel faster than the speed of light, shaping everything else outside. If Helen Keller lived, she would repeat her lines: "Alone we can do so little. **Together** we can do so much."

However, there is something still inherently dangerous here. Yes, once again! Sorry. This time it is even worse in terms of risk of harm compared to those triggered by 'not so innocent fairy tales.' And even though the sages who lived before warned us against this danger, it seems many societies have today forgotten about it. Our enemy is winning and we are losing as we are forgetting. So, let us analyze them once more here and repeat them to internalize.

Thanks to the fact being surrendered and bound in the sweetness of love relations, the thinkers like Socrates, Aristo and Plato have attracted our attention to what we need to pay attention to while flying like a catapult that blows us over our dreams.

Let us remember those times back then in Athens. Only free men who had completed their military service were allowed to vote on any legislation. This meant that only about a few of the population were actually able to vote. Women were not allowed to vote and subsequently possessed significantly fewer rights than men. These were not the only complaints against the early democracy of Athens. In the course of his writings, the philosopher Plato extensively examined what he considered serious dangers that resided within the system of democracy.

Van **Bryan**, a contributing author for Classical Wisdom, is an intrepid young writer after having studied classical literature as well as ancient and contemporary philosophy. For those who forget, he manages to raise a curiosity in today's dominant entertainment world to discover ancient thinking, lost civilizations, and strange mysteries that still puzzle us today. Let us experience together once again the power and people, the weapons and wisdom of the ancient world.

The numerous executions would give reason to doubt the system of Athenian democracy. However, there was a far more sinister nature to democracy. A calamity at the very heart of democracy, it would lead only to tyranny and subjugation.

Plato teaches us in his valuable book VIII of *The Republic,* when he begins to describe several stages of government that are intolerable, yet unavoidable. He predicts a society with an enormous socioeconomic gap, where the poor remain poor and the rich become richer off the blood and sweat of others. People subject to such ruling will consequently long for freedom and liberty. Plato argued that they then will use it as a battle cry against their oppressors, sparking a revolution

The looming danger lies exactly there: During times of transition, people can favor onemanship. They tend to rally behind one man, or a few men, whom they believe to be their savior. The people will lift this champion to great heights and anoint him with sacred responsibilities to bring liberty to the land.

1776 and the ten years following was a special era. In just a few years major events happened more or less at the same time: What was the most important document published in 1776? Most Americans would probably say The Declaration of Independence. But many would argue that Adam **Smith's** "The Wealth of Nations" had a bigger and more global impact, may forgetting about The French Revolution. This was a period of far-reaching social and political upheaval in France and its colonies beginning in 1789 and ending in 1799. The Revolution overthrew the monarchy, established a republic, catalyzed violent periods of political turmoil, and finally culminated in a dictatorship under a new leader. Napoleon brought many of its principles to areas he conquered in Western Europe and beyond. Inspired by liberal and radical ideas such as equality before the law, the Revolution made a profound impression on the course of modern history, influencing the decline of absolute monarchies while replacing them with republics and liberal democracies

"When the smoke clears the old regime -with no intention whatsoever for social transfer and uplifting others - will be gone and a democracy will be supplanted."

Plato had foreseen this. And while this is reminiscent of several historical revolutions, including the American revolution, Plato warns that the trouble only intensifies from here:

During the course of his writings Plato differentiates between necessary desires and unnecessary desires. Necessary desires are desires we cannot overcome, such as our desire for shelter and sustenance. Unnecessary desires are desires that we are able to overcome, yet refuse to. These desires include luxuries and lavish possessions. These types of desires are a result of a rapid influx of liberty into the population. Once we have tasted freedom, we become drunk off it. Plato predicts that the people will demand freedom at every turn, fighting any form of authority and demanding more liberty. We become obsessed with our freedom and become willing to sacrifice necessary things like social order and structure to attain it.

At this point, the newly appointed leaders become very nervous. It was so easy to depose their predecessors, so why not them?

Van **Bryan** summarizes this elegantly as below:

These democratic leaders will realize that they are only easily supported when there is a war that the people can rally behind. And so, the democratic leaders will unnecessarily become involved in violent affairs, creating wars to distract the people. To ensure their power, the leaders will create laws to bolster their position. The rulers will impose heavy taxes against the commoners to ensure they are unable or unwilling to fight back against this. And any who do oppose the leaders will be labeled as an enemy and persecuted as a spy. It is for this reason that there must always be some enemy combatant that the leader can cast blame upon.

Plato continues in his discussion by explaining that these leaders will eventually become unpopular, an unavoidable result. Those who once supported this ruling class begin to rebel against the would-be tyrant. At this point the citizens will try to get rid of whatever man is currently in office, either by exile or impeachment. If this is not possible, the ruler will inevitably crack down any opponents, including any political opposition.

Hated by the people, these leaders will request the presence of a body guard. And now he is a tyrant, the leader has no choice if he wishes to rule. Elected by the people, yet now he is protected from them. Plato predicts that this tyrant will appeal to the lowest form of citizen. He will make soldiers of the slaves and the degenerates. The tyrant will pay them to protect him from the ordinary citizens. And now the leader is a tyrant, born from democracy and propped up by the demand for liberty. And in our quest for liberty, we instead created a monster, Plato argues.

Plato's description of a democracy – and an economic belief system that is not focusing on growth enabling social transfer - is rather thought provoking. It gives us pause and forces us to examine our own government. In some countries, with an accelerating trend, could it be true that our leaders are the bullies and the political tyrants that Plato describes?

Does democracy lead to entangling wars for the benefit of the **ruling class**?

And are the people so subjugated by senseless laws and stiff taxes, that they are unable to resist in any **meaningful** way?

Perhaps.

History has shown a consistent pattern of subjugation, revolution and subjugation once again.

Plato predicted that democracy can be easily hi-jacked and could lead to nations being governed by bullies and brutes. Let us take a minute and think about this in calm.

Van **Bryan** emphasized that we are allowed to doubt Plato if we wish; stating rather ironically, that is a freedom we are allowed.

However, we are not doomed with an answer black or white. We can have a cultivated discussion around this:

On one side it was the political philosopher Thomas **Paine** who describe government as, "at best, a necessary evil". And if we are to think in this manner, then perhaps democracy is simply the least damaging form of government we have been able to create over the course of human existence. A thinly veiled tyranny is better than outright oppression.

Yet when we study the success of social welfare economic system and the role of democracy within those – good examples are provided by Nordic countries as well as German-speaking countries in general we witness the fruits of hard work both in labor and thinking. How long or how quick the path to the term Wirtschaftswunder (German: "economic miracle") was today depends on the selection of a rhetoric – that is motivated to unite for progress or divide for nostalgia.

To internalize the lessons learnt of Wirtschaftswunder, an expression referring to this phenomenon first used by *The Times* magazine in 1950, describing the rapid reconstruction and development of the economies of West Germany and Austria after World War II, we need to have a closer look why adopting an ordoliberalism-based social market economy has been important.

Whatever your opinions of democracy, American, Brazilian, Hungarian or otherwise, it is necessary to keep in mind these charges Plato has laid before us. And the next time we celebrate any national holiday for independence, let us keep in mind that a wise man and his supporters much before any of us once called to our attention the unavoidable and disastrous nature of the pursuit of liberty.

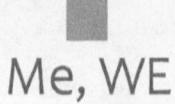

Me, WE

For many, who suffer an Alzeimer's disease surely prioritize huge concerns on the loss of independence and shorter survival over less important matters, such as the knowledge about how long our sun in our planet system will last let alone if we are able to pinpoint more precisely when it will burn out. Even though humanity never managed to escape the fact of its own mortality, we see more and more how we can deal with its implications. This requires a deeper understanding through time about ourselves and our universe. Every generation puts a little more air to our gigantic air-balloon lifting our consciousness higher, and every one of us plays his role within it, independent of how we subjectively find the meaning of our own existence in our own way of transcending death by attaching ourselves to permanent things that will outlast us, such as **love** for instance.

This book, then, shall be interpreted as a 'love letter' to those moments when our conscious and subconscious beliefs can be united, both visually and intrinsically to reach a point of everything is possible, especially when we are very down at the level of zero. To allow growth again. To thrive. To develop further.

But what could be the social side of this question that seems to be an individual?

Has art pioneered in this regard?

The idea of many new beginnings from the zero point gives us some clues called ZERO (zero) to revive the art world that has been stagnated by the destructive effects of the Second World

War. ZERO art movement is coming back to the exact time we need with the effect of the coronavirus epidemic today.

Two German artists; Otto Piene and Heinz Mack are two important architects of the ZERO movement that started in 1957 and deeply influenced the art world for the following ten years. This duo, which created in one of the countries most affected by the Second World War, has embarked on its arms to revive the art life that has come to a standstill in Germany, and sought a brand-new art, completely away from traditional methods. According to them, like Germany, which was almost rebuilt after the war, art should have started from the very beginning, from scratch. This could only be achieved by getting rid of traditional methods that form the basis of art such as paint, composition, figure, and using materials that have never been used before, in the light of technology and ever-evolving science.

So where and how do these new beginnings feed?

The efforts of many generations who lived before make this possible: Those in our lives who are dying, or who have died, teach us about the value of living. They remind us not to take our lives for granted, but to live each moment of life to its fullest, and to remember that our own small lives form of a part of a greater whole. Every new generation gets better opportunities fueled by the accumulation of wisdom and the advance of technology and innovative ways of societal togetherness: So how can we use this progress for easing the levels of individual stress and finding meaning?

At the end of the day, the game will not change, dice are thrown: there will be those close to death tomorrow, and facts will not matter...but for everyone else, there will be many many beginnings.

While the conditions of global confinement are brutal, it is also a burden on our shoulders to prevail over the conceptual war worshiping divide-rule enforced by very human hands.

Today, during the times of the coronavirus pandemic, the whole world follows daily and carefully how the growth of death tolls praise such solidarity, to keep our future connected. Nevertheless, we also witness, that there are countries driven by mentalities to break this solidarity by even politicizing death. They cover the real death tolls to conform with the 'outer world', as an expression of 'good governance'. This only proves that like positivity, negativity has his own perseverance too!

Most of today's ecological complications and natural imbalances arise from deep-seated social problems. In other words, present ecological problems cannot be deeply understood, much less resolved, without dealing with problems within our societies. To make this point more concrete: economic, ethnic, cultural, and gender conflicts, among many others, lie at the core of the most serious ecological dislocations we face today—apart from those caused by natural catastrophes.

Constantine **P. CAVAFY**, the Greek poet, born 1863 in today's Turkey, stabilized his place in Western Poetry by suggesting that the world can only change if everyone can change the configuration of the inner 'city' he or she consciously or non-consciously built at the first place. Clearly, we cannot trace many times exactly where misleading, limitations or negative forces stem from.

"Words are more powerful than perhaps any one suspects, and once deeply engraved in a child's mind, they are not easily eradicated."

May Sarton would emphasize.

Along our narrow road, the collision of the truth with that engravement makes all opaque. Yet we have the power to make an effort to find out and clear things. We can ask an old **friend**. We can get help. We can read or just have a walk in nature. Nobody knows all answers.

"Without darkness, nothing comes to birth. As without light, nothing flowers."

a good friend would suggest.

What we know for sure is that if we manage to overcome them, our way of looking will change thereafter toward reverence.

An example of such significant change can be found in Knut **Hamsun's** or Martin **Heidegger's** developmental inner cycles, manifested in the difference of their earlier political beliefs, and those in maturity. Even though in his younger years, Hamsun had leanings of an anti-egalitarian and racist bend, he has then pioneered psychological literature with techniques of stream of consciousness and interior monologue. He influenced many great authors such as Thomas **Mann**, Max **Frisch**, Franz **Kafka**, Stefan **Zweig**, Hermann **Hesse**, and Ernest Hemingway; and was awarded the Nobel Prize, for his creative, supportive, and deeply appreciative way of looking to the needs of human life. For Martin Heidegger, a famous thinker or Robert **Oppenheimer**, the father of the atom bomb, such a change was similar.

"In a total work, the failures have their not unimportant place" May Sarton would say.

Such a change would mean a far-reaching transformation of our prevailing mentality of domination into one of complementarity, in which we would see our role in the natural world as creative, supportive, and deeply appreciative of the needs of human-life but also nonhuman- life. Toward respect. Toward peace! From a world of hierarchy to peace, sterilized from illegitimate forces. May be, towards a world free from abuse, indoctrination, propaganda, domination. Many thought leaders expand our thoughts into such a peaceful possibility; a new beginning. Otto **Rank**, Jean-Paul **Sartre**, Oswald **Spengler**, Edward **Said** and, Noam **Chomsky**, just to name a few, hint us the entry doors for such a dream world.

The way human beings deal with each other as social beings is therefore crucial to addressing today's ecological crisis. Unless we clearly recognize this, we will surely fail to see that the hierarchical mentality and class relationships that so thoroughly permeate society give rise to the very idea of dominating the natural world.

The configuration of stars changes through time and our choice for activism contributes to redefining what we want from life, to feel better about ourselves, to find the balance between chaos and perfection in each of us.

If the cumulative weight of tragedy in our times has become too unbearable, I invite you to distance yourself from all negative sources of news for a while. Switch off your devices and anything that will distract you. And let us give ourselves the opportunity to rediscover a privileged mode of presence to the self, to others, to the sensible world, and finally to tear ourselves away from being absorbed by

DIVISION AND LIMITATION.

A COLLECTIVE WALK

NOW I BECOME MYSELF

One of the greatest things about discovering this office was the path it leads me down and doors it opened into new insights and findings that I otherwise might have never known. Like an article we read leads us to a new author or book. A conversation we have leaves us dig deeper into something or someone we've never heard of. A play on the radio inspires us to learn more about a business or topic being discussed. Similarly, this is an invitation for a collective walk. Let's enjoy a virtual tour in the architect's office:

From one angle, Damla's architecture office white interior, surrounded through an arch of olive trees, blends perfectly into rural Muğla's winding roads, stone walls, barns and summer camps. However, getting close, it becomes obvious something is unusual. The neatly trimmed garden, irrigated to stay emerald green, is mowed in different directions creating a sense of movement.

Architecture Office,
Damla SEVIL
2013

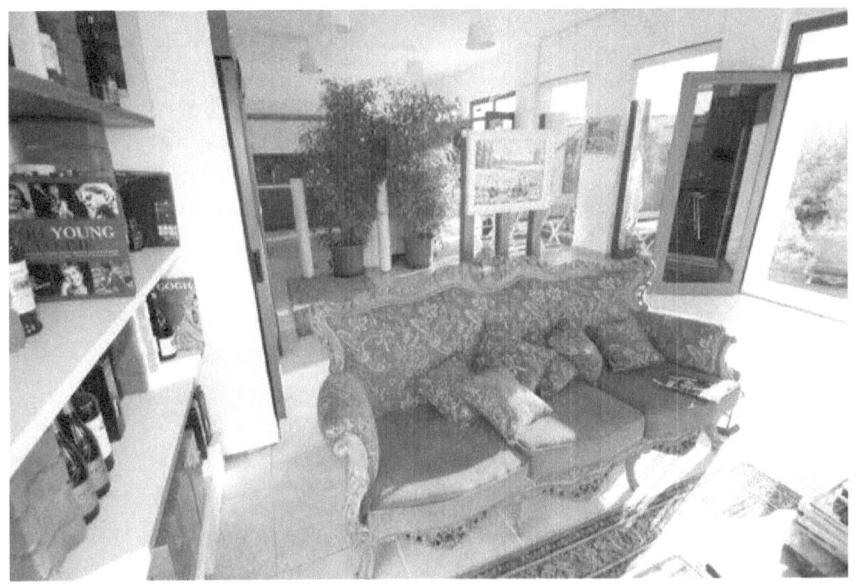

Image: Courtesy of the Architect. Muğla

All of us, in search of a new form of energy and a higher level of consciousness through wisdom and happiness, are headed independently but voluntarily towards the labyrinths of life.

Some of us, those closer to art and literature, can find pleasure in the observed and studied wisdom of the artists or writers, who lived, thought, and worked before us have a cheerful voice:

"Now I become myself. It's taken time, many years and places."

This book, for example, came to life when such two persons met each other. Not physically though, but through a closer co-understanding and sharing of something remarkable in each of them. Now **the inclusion** of a reader, in the *l'atelier* providing a natural spirituality in a quest for awakening, will surely initiate many many other beginnings.

L'atelier is a place where art completes nature to celebrate by lowering needless stress. It will inspire us in ecological restoration, and fostering peace and developing an aesthetic appreciation of natural evolution in all its diversity.

This diversity includes peer-production, free-speech and open access to diverse ideas. Yet, Damla's office is ongoing a change towards a more collaborative enterprise where ideas can be shared and developed with other creative individuals in the arts, sciences and economics with the general idea of looking at the world through a different lens.

In such a togetherness, participants will walk collectively through the garden of art and literature to meet others among the way. They will complement with their own capacities to produce a richer, creative, and developmental whole - not as a 'dominant' species but as a supportive one.

Consequently, this book invites similar minded visitors to come together for a tour and watch their effect of connectedness grow:

ART AND LITERATURE TOWARDS A WE-CULTURE aims at new mentality in its call for a collective effort to use art and literature for the support of National Health Services, in each country around the World.

Using the Zoom Meeting Code*, provided by this specific book, the idea lies first in creating a loop between three parties: an architect, an author and the reader, who is the observer but most significantly a self-interpreter with desires for a collective walk through the office: The reader will thus have a chance to volunteer in participating to a free webinar and can provide a-priori questions that will be answered during each week's 30 minutes Virtual-Visit-Webinar. Being able to meet with others online is breaking down geographical and cultural barriers and connecting people, who would normally never have the chance to meet, to communicate.

The author and the architect strongly believe that a small contribution can make a change to remind us of the importance of human relationships during extraordinary times.

Marcel **PROUST**, a sickly child who suffered from severe asthma attacks long before he became famous as a novelist and essayist to provide one of the greatest works of modernist fictions, loved mysterious moments. He loved to communicate with nature, with art, with life, in these `deep minutes' in which his entire being was concentrated. He, like many other, knew that joy is fundamental to growth. Only when we are in a pleasant state of experience, our body and brain work at our best.

Yet at the end of the day, we fade away as fast as the morning breaks. Death is closure. But life is possibility. If you are just alive, everything is open.

"This is to be celebrated!" he emphasized,

Our experience is only determined by us.

"Only through art," he noted, "we can enter the secret universe of another, the only journey in which we truly 'fly from star to star,' a journey that cannot be navigated by direct and conscious methods."

So, we only need to remember: There is a time for everything.

There is a time to drift on wide summer riddles, but there is also a time for snow and ice and shivers. That's the mysterious dynamic of the odyssey:

There is a time for truth and being together.

There is a time to go for walks in sunny, brittle weather.

So, we only need to remember:

Only living by the positive principle and respecting Nature, we can find our space in the cosmos of our minds, where we can grow

IN WEALTH,

WISDOM,

AND

HAPPINESS.

About the Author

Old-fashioned Master (ca.1500-) has walked a lot and pursuit various career paths, from an academic at the Institute for Economic Theory at Universities to a technician at the Engineering Institutions to a consultant for the Establishment. He never knew about failure and was always on the sunny side of his village, until he met the constraints of his comfort zone. Then he eventually realized that there are strong powers that underlay everything in life, which forces us to get curious and to learn by listening to those, who know or knew better, but who also interestingly expressed themselves better throughout history. As a travelogue he walked a lot and could live in different continents and saw the roots of his first name, uniting people together for a social goal, was validated through the creation of interconnected human bonds.

THE END
OF
THE BOOK

6

THE END

Athens, 17h05,

01 January 2019,

"TO BE a student in debt SUCKS. It makes you only live within a permanent dream to find a good recession-safe job."

he inhaled. Despite the one-hour delay, he was finally airborne, now in the middle of a 3-hour flight three thousand five hundred meters above ground, flying with the only airline that could take him home as quickly as possible. He tried to manipulate his mind, imagining the smell of soil and not to think about his father and what would happen to him by the time he would arrive at the hospital in a few hours.

He tried to manipulate his mind, imagining the smell of soil and not to think about his father and what would happen to him by the time he would arrive at the hospital in a few hours. Still, at unease, he was stuck in the movie he was watching on the couch in Paris the day before:

"It would seem that the respect for principle and the love of one's neighbor have become dysfunctional in this country of ours, and that all we have done, all that we have succeeded in accomplishing with our power is simply annihilating the hopes of the newborn countries in this world, as well as friends and enemies alike, that we're not humane, and that we do not live up to our agreements."

Luckily the plane was not in turbulence. The coffee was served on time, and the landing was due shortly. During the journey, he listened to classical music. However, he was still under the influence of the movie "The Godfather." Besides the movie, he was shocked to learn about its famous actor Marlon Brando, who rejected the Oscar award in 1973 for best actor to help turn the attention of the public to Wounded Knee Massacre. The actor did not even attend the ceremony. That night he had sent a young

Indian woman named Sacheen Littlefeather to give a speech to the awards ceremony on his behalf. The young Indian could not read the entire letter written by Brando on the stage.

"It's hard enough for children to grow up in this world. When Indian children watch television, and they watch films, and when they see their race depicted as they are in films, their minds become injured in ways we can never know."

Then he sighed. Still, he thought of his own family and family for a moment without regretting the most expensive last-minute flight ticket he had ever had to buy in this life unexpectedly a few hours ago. Unlike Brando, everything about him was ordinary. He sighed. His mind was still on Marlon Brando, and those who had had that Oscar awards 45 years ago:

"Recently there have been a few faltering steps to correct this situation, but too faltering and too few, so I, as a member in this profession, do not feel that I can as a citizen of the United States accept an award here tonight. I think awards in this country at this time are inappropriate to be received or given until the condition of the American Indian is drastically altered. If we are not our brother's keeper, at least let us not be his executioner. I would have been here tonight to speak to you directly, but I felt that perhaps I could be of better use if I went to Wounded Knee to help forestall in whatever way I can the establishment of a peace which would be dishonorable as long as the rivers shall run and the grass shall grow."

By the time he arrived at the hospital, it was 19:20, local time. As he entered inside through the glass doors and immediately saw everybody he knew in his family, who, unlike him, was luckily living in the same city. At that moment, all the family circled around his mother, trying to comfort her.

"I must have come just too late!" he thought instinctively.

A few seconds after, as soon as he could hug her mother, this time, she shed all her remaining tears on his shoulders.

"He is in a coma for the last 24 hours,"

his mother said.

"The doctors do not tell us anything and do not let anyone go past that door."

Taking advantage of that confusion, among everyone's gaze, and despite trying to stop him, he suddenly passed beyond the door without listening to anyone.

He moved forward into the first room in the hallway as he saw his father right there, motionless in the white, large bed, next to the doctors who surrounded him. The doctors, who saw his name on his business card, were surprised when they realized that someone dared to cross that door, someone of the patient's relative they never knew before who was neither a famous media name nor someone distinguished in the business world. A young student without a job. A straightforward, ordinary citizen, handing out a business card, not as a threat some extroverts would do, but because of respect to the profession. So, they looked at each other and eventually allowed him to stay next to his father without any further hassle. For fourteen days. Fourteen days in which he waited that his father would wake up. Yet, his father could not wake up and his consciousness did not come back. After 14 days he left everyone for good, without a chance to say good-bye.

Then he left the room, smiled at his awaiting mother:

"Smile for me. It will pass."

Her mother looked at him, showing a letter, trying to smile. There was the handwriting of his father, he wrote:

"Now, it is up to you to raise our child, which I know I cannot see even though I wanted it so much. My wish from you is to give our child the following letter if he would forget one day in the future. This letter is my will to him."

and added;

"If he solves the puzzle written on the paper

Every time defaults anew

My memory

To earths coming

The earths leaving

Who am I really?

and can grasp what I mean, he will never forget me and become the wisest person of his time."

* * *

ONCE the script was written, 'Jackie, The Master' did not know what to do next. He couldn't possibly hold it inside. It had to come out or it would burn him alive. Therefore, he immediately rushed to Jack and Jacqueline, who after reading it, both commented that here and there, there were some missing pieces.

They started to make some changes.

Yet in the end, they were a small group. They could not agree if they could potentially eliminate the domination of human by human alone and how deal with those ecological problems whose growing magnitude threatens the existence of a biosphere than can support advanced forms of life.

'Jackie, The Master' put it blantly:

"Yet, to ignore the need for these sweeping but eminently practical changes would be to let our ecological problems fester and spread to a point where there would no longer be any opportunity to resolve them."

Jacqueline continued:

"There are so many things that each of us wants right now. You love walking. The joy of walking transcends setting; it engages the mind as well as the spirit. Many walkers like you do not like there to be buildings in their way, and that's fine for them. Others of us just can't do without the buildings."

She added:

"To trigger a start is not enough, we need everyone to act together now. Yet this will not be possible. We will never change people who ignore their impact on the biosphere, yet alone those who cannot read. Of course, propaganda, allegories, and calls to action are not themselves action, and art that represents change or resistance does not necessarily affect change or resistance. Dealing with them singly is bowling alone.

There are different interpretations of the history: For some, many communities have shown themselves incapable or unwilling to understand and moreover adopt the universal values. Others, those who seemingly adapt them, possesses a will for domination, that justifies them to resist with limited resources available for them.

Art and power have always been begrudging bedfellows. It would be recipe for disaster, a guarantee that the anti-ecological society that prevails in most of the world today would blindly hurtle the biosphere as we know it to certain destruction."

raising her tone, for the first time since she broke up with 'Jackie, The Master'.

'Master, Jason' could not stand this tone and as soon as he replied:

"Love is stronger than all wars."

they all started to re-argue in a hypnotic state.

167

The book could never be published.

As a hand we feel for, that will never be joined,
it never reached its audience, leaving the puzzle

Every time defaults anew
My memory
To earths coming
The earths leaving
Who am I really?

unsolved.

"The saddest aspect of life right now is that science gathers knowledge faster than society gathers wisdom."

— Isaac Asimov, 1950

Ex-president of the *American Humanist Association*

"I would hope that those who are listening would not look upon this as a rude intrusion, but as an earnest effort to focus attention on an issue that might very well determine whether or not this country has the right to say from this point forward we believe in the inalienable rights of all people to remain free and independent on lands that have supported their life beyond living memory.

Thank you for your kindness and your courtesy to Miss Littlefeather. Thank you and good night."

— Marlon Brando, **1973**

Once Hollywood's most inscrutable star

"When will we learn? When will the people of the World, get up and say, enough is enough? God created us for fellowship. God created us so that we should form the human family, existing together because we were made for one another."

— Archbishop Desmond Tutu, **1984**

Nobel Peace Prize

"Is the public 20 years too late? Or is the artist 20 years early? This is where I am. My mission is to bring the people from one side to the other."

— Yoyo Maeght, **2010**

President of the Foundation Marguerite et Aimé Maegght

"All states should prioritize education system reforms country by country for the protection of a peaceful, non-violent human family. To change the cumbersome structure of education in the world, we need statemen who can be asked for an account in education for an education system that is accountable, questionable, and more efficient in terms of results."

— Cem Tanrıöver, **2020**

Artist, Writer

OUR INNER CITIES

Don!T let your child spin like your head is spinning!
Don't loose your mind.
Your dream, your inner cities,
A voice falls; always deep.

Don!T let your child spin like your head is spinning!
Read, sing.
Write, draw.
Your voice is falling deep...

Read: When you see man fall,
Write: Don't laugh!
Your voice is falling deep.
Don!T let your child spin like your head is spinning!

Read: The thing that tempt man to fall;
Write: Don't laugh, you and I, not free from temptation
Sing: Know from the weakness we stumble and fall
Draw: Don't laugh, you and I, not free from temptation
Your voice is falling deep.
Don!T let your child spin like your head is spinning!

Read: When you see man fall;
Write: Don't laugh. When you laugh at someone else's fall
Draw: Black, Purple, Green or White. Your voice is falling deep.
Don!T let your child spin like your head is spinning!

Read: enemy or friend, when you laugh: someone laughs,
Write: Don't laugh when see man fall. Don't open a way.
Sing: Because to laugh and not to learn to internalize
Your voice is falling deep.
It is to make the same mistake of your enemy!
Your voice is falling deep.
It is to make the same mistake of your friend!
Your voice is falling deep.
It is to make the same mistake yourself!
Don!T let your child spin like your head is spinning

Don!T let your child spin like your head is spinning!
Read, sing.
Write, draw.
Don't let it fall into the deep.

MANY MANY BEGINNINGS
By Cem TANRIOVER
05 May 2020

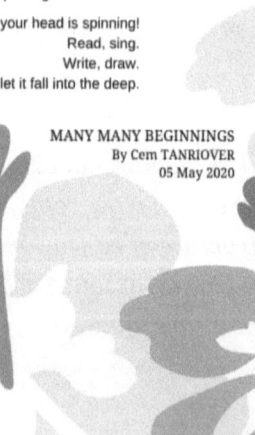

THE END

ABOUT THE AUTHOR

The author Cem Tanrıöver (1976) has pursuit various career paths, from an academic at the Institute for Economic Theory at the University of Freiburg, Germany, to Eurocrat at the European Institutions such as The European Space Agency ESA, the European Border and Coast Guard Agency Frontex, The European Organisation for the Safety of Air Navigation Eurocontrol to a Silicon Valley consultant for SmartOrg, Palo Alto. He never knew about failure and was always on the sunny side of the street, until he met the constraints of his comfort zone. Then he eventually realized that there are strong powers that underlay everything in life, which forces us to get curious and to learn by listening to those, who know or knew better, but who also interestingly expressed themselves better throughout history.

As a travelogue he could live in different continents working closely with international artists, psychologists, and architects. He was constantly on the move. He visited many countries, and dozens of cities. He had used a wide variety of modes of transportation—from planes to fast-trains to ships to donkeys. He traveled for pleasure and business. In general, travel was one of the major components of his dislocation, with no real home, no real country. The ease with which he had moved around the world only enhanced his ability to avoid permanent connections, to escape responsibilities, and to remain completely unknown and un-judged. In this sense he was a refugee of sorts until he saw the roots of his first name -from Arabic origin for uniting people together for a social goal, was validated through the timeless creation of interconnected human bonds.

OTHER BOOKS

AMAZON   https://www.amazon.com/gp/product/B089M433Q6

CONTACT

LINKED IN   http://www.linkedin.com/in/cem-tanriover-dipl-vw-a9426412
WEB   http://www.cemtanriover4.wixsite.com/website
FACEBOOK   htpps://www.facebook.com/authorcemtanriover

ABOUT INSPIRATION

Imagine spending and entire professional life-time studying cuneiform clay tablets from 5,300 B.C. onward. What about being faced with the task of cataloguing 74-5,000 of them? Then imagine being there when someone makes a precious find. Just imagining it seems extraordinary and it must take an extraordinary person to do this. Muazzez Çığ is one of the few rare people who have been in just that position.

Born in 1914, Muazzez Ilmiye Itil's father was a teacher and had especially wanted a daughter who he wanted to have learn French and study the violin - hence the name Ilmiye, which means 'knowledge.' Her parents on both sides were from the Crimea originally and migrated to Turkey. Her mother's family settled in Bursa and her father's in Merzifon. However, after the Greek army invaded Izmir and advanced towards Ankara, the family moved to Corum where they thought they would be safer.

How did Muazzez Hanim become interested in Sumerology? She and a close friend, Hatice Kizilyay, had completed teacher training and were going on to university and she wanted to study French, she could not, however, because those classes were already full. Her advisor then suggested Hittitology, Sumerology and Archaeology. The two of them had never heard of these but gamely decided to pursue them.

The 1930s was a time when a number of prominent German Jewish scholars took refuge in other countries because of the rise of the Nazis. Quite a number of them came to Turkey including B. Lansberger and his student, Hans Guterbock, who became a world-renowned Hittite scholar. Undoubtedly this was an exciting time with plenty of stimulus.

The 1930s was also a time of reform under the leadership of Ataturk who particularly liked to encourage women. Although Turkey was far from recovering from the War of Independence and lacked capital and an industrial base, the government took on the burden of setting up needed industry and educational opportunities. But we see at the same time the start of businesses that today still dominate the Turkish business world. As often happens, in a society with a large proportion of uneducated people, women who do have an education can generally secure a good job.

After finishing her studies, she along with her friend Hatice Kizilyay was appointed to work in 1940 at the Istanbul Archaeological Museums and spent the whole of her professional life there. The same year Kemal Çığ, the director of Topkapi Palace Museum, and she were married. She and others were responsible for the cuneiform tablets. It is what some would call this armchair archaeology, because she didn't need to take part in excavations. Her material had already been collected and stored in the Museum although lacking storage drawers and cupboards. These came later. She has published a number of books ranging from one on the Hittites, whose language she originally set out to learn to Ataturk's thoughts. She is after all counted among the group of women whom the Turkish leader befriended and saw to their education.

She was working at a time when the great Sumerologist Samuel Noah Kramer was producing as many translations of Sumerian literary texts as possible. Excavations in the second half of the 19th century had produced innumerable tablets, many of which were deposited in Istanbul thanks to Osman Hamdi Bey, who founded the Istanbul Archaeology Museums.

When Çığ talks about the conditions in which she worked, you wonder why she continued. Salaries were low, appointments were made on a personal basis, no budget from the government for anything extra such as publishing books, storage cupboards had to be made by the museum staff and compared with the early start of museums and museology in the West, Turkey lagged very far behind. In fact only very recently have museum studies courses been added to university curriculum. Certainly Çığ had none but then she was a philologist more than anything else and had studied to be a teacher.

Çığ is a staunch secularist and outspoken in her opinions but found herself taken to court two years ago at the age of 92 not for her secular beliefs but because of her writing in which she took on the turban/veil issue. Conservative Muslims believe that women should keep their hair covered while secularists believe wearing them should continue to be banned. According to Çığ and research that she had been carrying out for several years, Sumerian women who were priestesses and offered sexual services were the first to wear veils. An Izmir lawyer had her taken to court on the grounds that she was fomenting religious hatred. It took about one hour for her to be acquitted by the court in which she appeared.

Muazzez İlmiye Çığ over the course of her lifetime has written 14 books; she reportedly only learned to use a computer when she was 85. She never seems to stop or slowdown.

On June 20, 2020 she celebrated her 107th birthday.

We hereby thank you Gül Demir - Niki Gamm for this article published on 15 November 2008

HÜRRİYET NEWSPAPER.

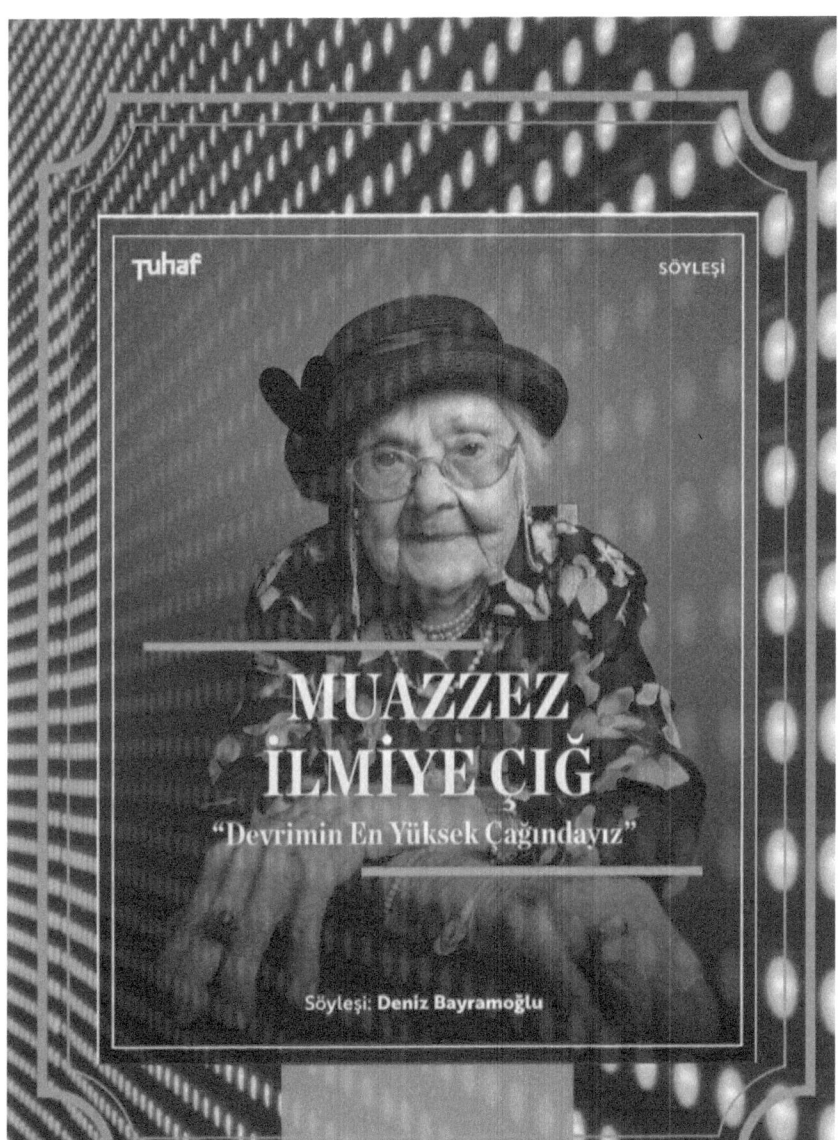

MUAZZEZ
İLMİYE ÇIĞ
"Devrimin En Yüksek Çağındayız"

Söyleşi: **Deniz Bayramoğlu**